HYBRID HOMESCHOOLING

HYBRID HOMESCHOOLING

A Guide to the Future of Education

Michael Q. McShane

ROWMAN & LITTLEFIELD
Lanham • Boulder • New York • London

Published by Rowman & Littlefield
An imprint of The Rowman & Littlefield Publishing Group, Inc.
4501 Forbes Boulevard, Suite 200, Lanham, Maryland 20706
www.rowman.com

6 Tinworth Street, London SE11 5AL, United Kingdom

Copyright © 2021 by Michael Q. McShane

All rights reserved. No part of this book may be reproduced in any form or by any electronic or mechanical means, including information storage and retrieval systems, without written permission from the publisher, except by a reviewer who may quote passages in a review.

British Library Cataloguing in Publication Information Available

Library of Congress Control Number: 2020950815

ISBN 978-1-4758-5796-2 (cloth)
ISBN 978-1-4758-5797-9 (pbk.)
ISBN 978-1-4758-5798-6 (electronic)

To Mom and Dad, now Grammy and Papa,
who taught me more than any school ever did.

No man is an island entire of itself; every man is a piece of the continent, a part of the main.

—John Donne

CONTENTS

Acknowledgments ix

Introduction 1

1 An Overview of Homeschooling 11
2 What Is Hybrid Homeschooling? 29
3 Focus on the Families 43
4 Teaching in a Hybrid Model 57
5 The Power of Policy 71
6 The Process of Innovation 89

Conclusion 105

Appendix: So You Want to Hybrid Homeschool? 117

Bibliography 123

Index 129

About the Author 131

ACKNOWLEDGMENTS

Writing a book like this is a leap of faith. To tell the stories of hybrid homeschoolers, an author has to hope that they will actually talk to him. I am eternally indebted to the people who took time out of their busy days and hectic lives to talk to me about their experiences.

Particularly, I would like to thank Josh and Rebecca Good, Ben Harris, Jeremiah Behling, Martha Herndon, Allison Morgan, Jim Falcotti, and Betsy Springer for not only agreeing to speak to me, but also connecting me to the teachers and families that they knew. During a global pandemic, they went out of their way to set up video calls with groups, make introductions, and follow up to make sure that folks would talk to me.

I have developed the ideas expressed in this book during the course of more than two years in my *Forbes* column; at my employer EdChoice's blog; in briefs written for the American Enterprise Institute; and during podcasts, radio interviews, and panel conversations. I'd like to thank all of those who gave me feedback in those forums. They helped refine and improve my thinking on the topic.

I owe a particular debt of gratitude to Kathleen Carroll, who meticulously edited the manuscript, offering an unfathomable number of changes and improvements. If you happen upon something particularly insightful, it is probably because of a recommendation of hers. If you find something dumb, that is all me.

I'd also like to thank the great folks at Roman & Littlefield, including Tom Koerner and Carlie Wall, who have been wonderful collaborators on numerous projects, and hopefully more in the future.

I'd also like to recognize and thank my friends and colleagues at EdChoice, particularly Paul DiPerna and Robert Enlow, who have been incredibly supportive throughout this entire process and jumped in at a late stage to read a draft of the manuscript. They kept a couple of clangors from getting to print. I'd also like to thank Jacob Vinson for his graphic design help.

Finally, I will never be able to adequately thank my family for their love and support. This includes my parents, to whom this book is dedicated, who always made sure to ask how my book was going and were willing to listen to me prattle on about it, and my dear wife and beloved daughter, who make my life worth living.

INTRODUCTION

It's a rare sixty-degree November Saturday in 2019 at the College Boulevard Activity Center in suburban Kansas City. This massive patchwork of athletic facilities, with baseball diamonds, tennis courts, and a soccer field, is operated by the Olathe Public Schools.

On Friday nights in the fall, sixty-five hundred fans fill the football stadium bleachers to support one of the district's large public high schools. But on this Saturday afternoon, the seats are only about one-third full. Even with the smaller crowd, the day has the typical trappings of a high-stakes high school football game: The stadium's sound system is blasting Bruce Springsteen's "Born in the USA" and the most recent pump-up song by pop-rock group Fall Out Boy; the sun is shining; and the cheerleaders are practicing lifts and tightening the red bows in their hair. The only thing that looks out of place is the sea of navy blue and white stars, which, as it turns out, are liberally borrowed from the New England Patriots. The team logo is on flags and t-shirts, which is a head-scratcher until it becomes clear that the home team is also called the Patriots and has adopted the pro team's logo and colors as its own. That's the only way to get away with that kind of thing here in the heart of Chiefs country.

I take my seat in the metal bleachers on the fifteen-yard line near the visiting team's end zone. The pregame warmup fires up in the usual fashion. The home team runs out through a gauntlet of cheerleaders, the announcer says a brief prayer, a young woman sings the national anthem, and the teams line up and kick off the ball to start the game.

In the bleachers, students from the home team are chatting about homecoming. Apparently one young man doesn't want to go, and his friends are trying to convince him otherwise. The announcer comes on the PA system during a break in the action to let us know that parents are selling chili dogs at the concession stand. A supporter in front of me is wearing a t-shirt that reads, "I'm a football dad. We don't do that Keep Calm thing."

Not two minutes into the first quarter, one of the home team's running backs breaks right around the visitor's defensive line and bursts through into the secondary, outflanking the linebackers and chugging toward the corner of the end zone. Instinctively, I stand up, with the fans around me, and shout for him to keep running as he outlasts his last pursuer and bursts into the end zone. The crowd goes wild.

As a student, a teacher, and a general fan of high school athletics, I've been to at least a hundred high school football games—but never one like this. The game is remarkable because of how utterly normal it is. It's just like the games I've seen in big and small stadiums throughout the country, from the Catholic school powerhouses of Washington, D.C., to the speed factories of rural Louisiana. The only difference is the teams themselves.

The "home" team, Christ Preparatory Academy, hails from a local hybrid homeschool program, where children attend formal classes three days a week and are homeschooled the other two. The visitor, Lighthouse Christian, from Springfield, Missouri, isn't even a school at all, but rather a collection of homeschooled students whose parents banded together to sponsor six different competitive sports programs, including the Chargers football team playing today. And the game, which sounds like some sort of one-off stunt, is actually the latest in a string of big games for these programs, which are ranked number one and number two in the National Homeschool Football Association.

Twenty years ago, there would have been no such game. But in recent decades, homeschooling has become more visible, more popular, and more organized throughout the United States. And little did anyone in the stadium know, its numbers were about to explode. As we sat and watched that game, a respiratory virus was mutating deep in the industrial heartland of China and preparing to make a jump from animals to humans. That virus, now known as COVID-19, would rip through China before making its way to Europe and the United States during the first few months of 2020. By April 1, every school district in the United States would be closed. Tens of millions of Americans would be out of work. Vast swaths of the country would be locked down, with citizens confined to their homes for all but essential ventures outside.

School closures due to COVID-19 prompted the largest experiment in home-based learning in our nation's history. In just a few short weeks' time, schools closed, and any education students received had to be delivered to them at home. Teachers used to supervising groupwork and delivering lectures were instead sending e-mails and holding videoconferences, and figuring out how to connect with students while developing new online-friendly lessons overnight. Some were successful; others fell short. In any event, it was up to parents to keep up kids' momentum. Suddenly, without warning or a choice in the matter, every family in America was schooling at home.

This presented a challenge to schools and districts. How could they rapidly pivot to providing education to students at home? Some responded better than others: An estimated one in five schools offered "rigorous" remote instruction that resembled in-classroom instruction by the end of the school year, according to the Education Response Longitudinal Survey developed by Nat Malkus, Cody Christensen, and Jessica Schurz of the American Enterprise Institute. An additional two in five offered what they deemed "perfunctory instructional programs." As for the rest, well, students and families were on their own.[1]

One group was, by design, well prepared for this sort of educational model: hybrid homeschoolers, who blend in-person learning in part-time programs with parent-led studies at home. During the long months of the spring of 2020, when everyone was staying home all the time, these families could draw on longstanding partnerships with teachers, established homeschooling structures, setups, and supplies, and years of experience in teaching their children.

By the time the summer of 2020 rolled around, schools and districts throughout the United States, facing an uncertain return to classrooms as the pandemic continued its spread, were even contemplating a hybrid homeschooling model for the fall to abide by social-distancing guidelines. The New York City Department of Education, the nation's largest public school district, announced that most of its 1.1 million students would only attend class one to three days each week and complete the rest of their learning at home. Districts elsewhere prepped in-person and remote learning plans, readying for anticipated rolling closures to curb likely outbreaks in the fall and winter.

It seems every family in the United States is now hybrid homeschooling, if not by choice, then at least with some warning. This volume arrives at an urgent moment, with context that can demystify the practice and reveal its unique challenges and strengths. The chapters in this book describe hybrid homeschooling and how its various models work, as well as why parents and educators choose to do schooling in this way. We'll explore how these hybrid programs fit within the broader landscape of our system of education and build on the history of homeschooling. And we'll discuss the policies that promote or thwart hybrid homeschooling and ask what can it teach us about educational innovation.

But first, a working definition. While chapter 2 goes into greater depth about exactly what is and is not hybrid homeschooling, the quick criteria for identifying a hybrid homeschooling program is that it is *regular*, *substantial*, and *structured*. That is, students attend a traditional brick-and-mortar school at regular intervals, for a substantial period of time, in a program that is structured to cater to homeschooling families. There are long traditions of homeschool co-ops, correspondence courses, online schools, and public-school districts that offer classes a la carte. While similar to hybrid homeschools in many ways, they are excluded from study here.

To tell the story of hybrid homeschooling we will crisscross the country, hearing from educators and families from the plains of Texas to the mountains of Colorado, from our nation's political capital in Washington, D.C., to its entertainment capital of Los Angeles. We will talk to representatives from traditional public schools that offer hybrid homeschool programs, public charter hybrid homeschools, and private hybrid homeschools. In a time of polarization and conflict between different schooling sectors, we will find broad similarities in what attracts families and educators to hybrid homeschooling in all kinds of schools. We will hear from representatives from religious schools and nonreligious schools, schools with progressive pedagogical models, and schools with traditional pedagogical models. As a movement, hybrid homeschooling is as varied as the people who opt to do it. It's not wedded to any one philosophical, religious, or pedagogical approach. But before we get there, it is important to understand where the American education system stands today.

THE AMERICAN EDUCATION SYSTEM, EXPLAINED

Imagine a triangle with 50 million children at the base and one nation at the apex. This is the public education system. As we train our attention from the bottom to the top, the various levels of educational delivery and management get progressively smaller. At the base: the 50 million children enrolled in public elementary or secondary schools in the United States. Up one level: the 3.2 million teachers who teach them. Up another: the 91,300 traditional public schools where they go to school. Jump up another level and count the 13,600 school districts that manage those schools. Then we reach the fifty states in the union whose constitutions enshrine the right to education and spell out its management, and finally we reach the peak, our one country.

The American education system is enormous and diverse, from massive school systems in our nation's major cities educating hundreds of thousands of children to tiny rural districts with less than 200 students. Throw in another 6 million students attending some 32,000 private schools, 3 million students attending some 7,200 public charter schools, and the 1.7 million children educated at home and you've got the entire picture.

It's also expensive: The United States spends approximately $700 billion on education each year in federal, state, and local tax dollars—second only to the military in total public investment. It works out to about $15,400 per student per year, on average.[2] That is an almost threefold increase in inflation-adjusted dollars since the 1970s and makes the United States one of highest-spending nations in the world when it comes to education.[3]

Despite that investment, many families are not happy with the education their children receive. For years, we have studied this phenomenon at EdChoice, a nonprofit that conducts and disseminates research about school-choice policies in the United States, where I am director national of research. According to the 2019 Schooling in America Survey, 67 percent of public-school parents said that they were "very" or "somewhat" satisfied with their child's education. This compares to 76 percent of homeschooling parents, 77 percent of charter-school parents, and 79 percent of private-school parents.[4] Consider the number of families represented by one-third of public-school respondents in our survey. Tens of millions of parents are not satisfied with their child's education.

The American education system is also rife with conflict. The vast majority of education funding comes from municipal and state tax dollars, and districts are managed by local school boards that residentially assign students to schools; therefore, most students' educational programs are dictated by where they live and who happens to be on the school board, and families who want something other than what is on offer are largely out of luck. According to such a system, conflicts about standards, curriculum, reading lists, and more are inevitable. Anyone wishing to offer an option outside of that system must rely on private funding or fight in the political sphere for financial support. This is the hotly contested realm of public charter schools and school voucher programs, which provide public tax dollars to families to attend private schools.

Battles between the local leaders in charge and the families whose children attend the schools they manage have a long history. Starting in the late 1830s, "Dagger John" Hughes, the Catholic archbishop of New York, clashed with leaders who operated "public" schools that read from the Protestant Bible, sang Protestant hymns, and taught from explicitly anti-Catholic and anti-immigrant texts. Hughes pushed to end the poor treatment of Catholic students and for Catholic schools to get the same funding that New York state had previously paid to other religious schools. When the legislature decided to ban funding to all religious schools instead of extend it to Catholic schools, a mob looted his house.[5] This sort of sentiment wasn't just in New York; in Philadelphia, the 1844 Nativist Riots started concerning rumors that Catholics might try to get the Bible removed from public schools or, saints preserve us, have the Catholic Bible read in class.

Clashes, albeit thankfully peaceful ones, continue to percolate throughout the county regarding a variety of issues related to public education, from how science is taught, to how history is taught, to what books should be read in literature classes, to how delicate topics like human sexuality should be taught. And this is just in the classroom. Sit in on a school board meeting when attendance boundaries are looking to be redrawn or a teacher contract is being renegotiated and some real sparks will fly.

Even when entirely independently financed, both private schools and homeschools are controversial as well. One frequent allegation: Withdrawing students from "common" public schools removes both financial resources and engaged families. Students would better serve the common good if they remained in public schools, the argument goes. Homeschools, in particular, are looked at suspiciously, with many commenters seeing them as a Trojan horse for political and religious indoctrination or, even worse, child abuse.

There are other problems with a system rooted in neighborhood schools. It is tough to look at the traditional public sector of the U.S. education system and not see a system that is fundamentally unequal. By linking school attendance with where children live, the school system reinforces residential segregation. Research has shown repeatedly that higher-quality schools drive up home prices,[6] which means that most top-flight public schools are available only to the children of parents who can purchase a wildly expensive home in the right catchment area. And all of this is outside of the lasting scars on our residential landscape from such public policies as redlining, where cities actively prevented African Americans from purchasing homes outside of specific areas, and the racist business practices of real estate agents and banks, who even today offer different housing stock and mortgage terms to African Americans. Linking school attendance to where children live reinforces these patterns, too.

There are reasons for people to look to do something different in education, both within and outside of the traditional system. Hybrid homeschooling is an example of one different approach.

It is important to be clear at this point that this book is not trying to sell hybrid homeschooling as a solution to everything that ails the U.S. education system. For reasons obvious to some readers already—and which will become obvious to everyone else as this book progresses—hybrid homeschooling is not for everyone.

So, one might ask, why the subtitle "A Guide to the Future of Education"? Fair question. At a basic level, if even a small percentage of American families decide, whether spurred by the coronavirus or something else, to give hybrid homeschooling a try, that represents an enormous number of children. Given the size and scope of the U.S. system, even if 2 percent of American families opted to become hybrid homeschoolers, they'd be educating more than 1 million students. That's enough to fill Arrowhead Stadium in Kansas City thirteen times.

But the likely future growth of the practice isn't what prompted me to write this book. Hybrid homeschooling represents the future of education not because it is popular, but because of the questions it asks about how we educate children and organize schools. What does it mean for schools to be communities? How can parents partner with schools to create institutions that reflect their desires and values? How can schools best use the limited time and resources available to them to maximize student learning? How can we make teaching a more enjoyable job? How do we promote educational innovation that solves important problems in a responsible way? Every school wrestles with these questions—or ought to. Looking at how hybrid homeschooling answers them can help traditional schools, whether public or private, think through their own responses.

THE BOOK AHEAD

This volume is divided into three sections. Section one begins with an overview of homeschooling. Before we talk about hybrid homeschooling, we should understand homeschooling in general. Chapter 1 traces the history of homeschooling, its scope and its scale, and what research tells us about who homeschools and what effects homeschooling has on students. It also gives airtime to common criticisms.

Chapter 2 is devoted entirely to explaining hybrid homeschooling. The definition and reality of the practice can be fuzzy because different schools and sectors use hybrid homeschooling in different ways. It is important to establish what is being studied here, while acknowledging the cases sitting right at the edges that could be reasonably included or excluded. The threefold definition of *regular*, *substantial*, and *structured* interaction with a school program is the guiding criteria for what is included. This chapter also looks at the historical antecedents for hybrid homeschooling and the limited research that has been conducted on them thus far.

In the second section, we'll explore hybrid homeschooling from the perspective of those that participate in it. Before and during the coronavirus lockdowns, I interviewed almost one hundred educators and families, both individually and in "focus group" style convenings, to hear about their experiences. Chapter 3 features parents' voices. Why do they do it? What have been some of the challenges? How have their children benefited?

Chapter 4 features the voices of educators. How do these schools get started? How did teachers and school leaders get involved? How are their roles different from those at other schools where they have taught? What is it like working so closely with parents? Educators were forthcoming in discussing the problems that hybrid homeschooling solves for them and the challenges it creates. These discussions are insightful on their own and also spark questions about how hybrid homeschooling might scale up.

That leads to the third section, where we'll step back and look at hybrid homeschooling within the context of the U.S. education system writ large. Chapter 5 dives into the policies that can either nurture or thwart hybrid homeschooling. From state homeschool laws and private-school regulations to part-time funding and charter school authorization rules, often seemingly unrelated policy decisions can have a big impact on hybrid homeschools. For example, school funding regulations directly shape what public hybrid homeschools look like. School choice programs have the potential to promote more hybrid homeschooling but have to cope with a skeptical audience. In sum, policy is the water in which hybrid homeschools swim. It can be rough or smooth.

Chapter 6 looks at education more broadly and asks what hybrid homeschooling can tell us about innovation. Actors both within and outside of education have pushed for improvement for more than a century and, more often than not, been disappointed with the results. Will hybrid homeschooling meet the same fate? Its laser-like focus on solving the specific problems of a small but substantial population bodes well. Rather than try and remake the entire education system, hybrid homeschools start small. They knuckle down on relieving specific irritations of teachers and families. Will that be able to scale? Perhaps or perhaps not, but the lessons it teaches us can apply to others hoping to innovate.

This book concludes with an appendix designed for those who want to pursue hybrid homeschooling. This section, and the book as a whole, was inspired by learning just how many people might be interested. Like many great things in life, I became aware of this entirely by accident.

Forbes has an online dashboard for its contributors that tracks page views by day. As someone who generally writes sleepy education policy columns, seeing the graph line pass a thousand or two thousand views is a cause for celebration.

On May 21, 2018, I published a column titled "Is Hybrid Homeschooling the Wave of the Future?" It was based on an interviewed I had conducted for my *Cool Schools* podcast, where I talked to Keri Beckman of the Regina Caeli school network. I put some data about homeschooling in there, described the model, and talked about some of the policy implications, and I hit post.

I have never experienced such a response. The pageview tracker went nuts. It didn't take long for it to exceed one hundred thousand views. For months, I got e-mails from parents interested in pursuing a hybrid home-school education for their child.

Clearly, I hit a nerve.

The response to that column is the genesis for this book. So, let's get to it.

NOTES

1. Nat Malkus, Cody Christensen, and Jessica Schurz, *School District Responses to the COVID-19 Pandemic: Round Six, Ending the Year of School Closures*. Washington, D.C.: American Enterprise Institute, 2020.

2. National Center for Education Statistics, "Table 236.55: Total and Current Expenditures per Pupil in Public Elementary and Secondary Schools: Selected Years, 1919–20 through 2016–17." *Digest of Education Statistics*, 2019, https://nces.ed.gov/programs/digest/d19/tables/dt19_236.55.asp (accessed October 20, 2020).

3. Organization for Economic Cooperation and Development (OECD), "Education at a Glance: OECD Indicators." *Online Education Database*, https://www.oecd.org/unitedstates/CN%20-%20United%20States.pdf (accessed October 20, 2020); see also National Center for Education Statistics, "Table 605.10: Gross

Domestic Product per Capita and Expenditures on Education Institutions per Full-Time Equivalent (FTE) Student, by Level of Education and Country: Selected Years, 2005 through 2016." *Digest of Education Statistics*, 2019, https://nces.ed.gov/programs/digest/d19/tables/dt19_605.10.asp (accessed October 20, 2020).

4. Paul DiPerna, Andrew D. Catt, and Michael Shaw, *2019 Schooling in America Survey: Public Opinion on K–12 Education, Busing, Technology, and School Choice*. Indianapolis, IN: EdChoice, 2019. Available at https://www.edchoice.org/wp-content/uploads/2019/10/2019-9-Schooling-in-America-by-Paul-Diperna-Andrew-Catt-and-Michael-Shaw-1.pdf (accessed October 20, 2020).

5. William J. Stern, "How Dagger John Saved New York's Irish," *City Journal* (Spring 1997), https://www.city-journal.org/html/how-dagger-john-saved-new-york%E2%80%99s-irish-11934.html (accessed October 20, 2020).

6. Abbigail J. Chiodo, Ruben Hernandez-Murillo, and Michael T. Owyang, "Nonlinear Effects of School Quality on House Prices." *Federal Reserve Bank of St. Louis Review* 92, no. 3 (May/June 2010): 185–204.

1

AN OVERVIEW OF HOMESCHOOLING

Julia Fuller spoke matter-of-factly.

"I've fostered over 100 children," she said, almost as an aside.

It's a warm April day on the far outskirts of Kalamazoo, Michigan, where Fuller has raised children, both biological and adopted, and shepherded the care and education of dozens more as a long-standing foster parent.

"How many children did you homeschool?"

"Twelve," she remembered. "The state won't let you homeschool foster children, but they did give me a waiver to homeschool one, because she was so behind in her credits. She graduated ahead of schedule."

I struggled to keep writing as she spoke because I was so gobsmacked by the stories she was telling me. Most were just nouns and verbs. No back-patting, flowery language. She talked about providing life-altering opportunities to children as if she was telling me what she was buying at the grocery store or had for dinner last night.

Each of these stories, humbly told, showed Fuller stepping forward at a crucial moment to reshape a child's future. One of her children was so far ahead of his peers at age thirteen that she had him take a standardized English exam that can confer college credits. He scored high enough to earn six credits in an afternoon. He is fully grown now, works full-time, and is leading a happy life. One of her adopted children had been classified as "mentally retarded" and told that she would never master complex subjects or ever live on her own. After Fuller dropped by a class and saw her elementary-age daughter being taught single-digit multiplication and single-syllable words, she withdrew the girl from school and started teaching her at home on the family farm. That child went on to graduate high school and complete several college classes, and is living a successful life as a young adult.

Fuller challenged assumptions about not only what children could and couldn't do, but also what she as a parent could and couldn't do. Why not see if an accelerated thirteen-year-old could earn college credit? Why not just start educating her daughter at home? To Fuller and thousands of other boundary-breaking parents, the purpose of school supersedes its structure. In this sort of thinking, every aspect of learning is determined by what works best for students and families, not what is currently available.

Plenty of families have opted out of their local schools and taken over their children's educations—while still far from the norm, parent-led homeschooling has been with us for decades, and the best estimates show it has been growing in recent years. But Fuller's children are engaged in something even less common: a hybrid homeschool program. She leads and substantially controls the content, pacing, and activities of each of her children's educations, but they are also enrolled in elective classes through their local school district, Gull Lake Community Schools.

Michigan's homeschooling regulations allow students to enroll in nonessential courses as local district policies allow; a district-run program called the Gull Lake Virtual Partnership provides such courses for students throughout Kalamazoo County and neighboring communities, homeschool or not. Kids and parents can pick and choose from a public-school elective program menu, rounding out their core activities at home, and state funding pays the bill.

Gull Lake has actively sought to provide such opportunities. The district's hybrid homeschooling pitch to her was straightforward: "We'll pay for your horseback riding lessons, we'll pay for your dance lessons," she recalled. "They got thousands of homeschoolers to sign up."

Indeed, several hundred homeschool students enroll each year, including two of Fuller's children. She drives forty miles each way so they can participate, but to her, it's worth it. "I used to put out a lot of money for sports and for dance," she said. "With a lot of kids, that adds up." But it wasn't just money, it was time. Now, these enrichment activities can take place during the day so, as she put it, "I'm not wasting every night driving around" from pillar to post.

She also saw a host of benefits for her children. Some were tangible. Her kids have been able to get dual enrollment credits, which allow high school students to earn college credit while completing their diploma. In Michigan, motivated students can earn enough credits to graduate with an associate's degree, at no cost to them. In addition, they have had access to music lessons, a wildly popular "field trip" class that takes students on trips to Chicago and Indianapolis and other popular educational destinations, and horseback riding.

But some were intangible, like making new friends and meeting students with differences in the inclusive classes that her children have taken with their peers from throughout the region. "If you're in public school in seventh grade, you're friends with other seventh graders. That's not true in the partnership. Dance, for example, is grades five through twelve," she said. She also saw benefits for students who needed extra help, or those with autism and students with ADHD.

As she commented,

> We enjoy the best of both worlds by attending the partnership. We interact with many like-minded children and adults during lessons and field trips. Children with physical, emotional, or cognitive challenges have a parent always nearby to assist or intervene without judgement from peers or instructors. Educational growth occurs best in a stress-free environment where each student is able to actualize his or her own potential.

UNDERSTANDING HOMESCHOOLING

Fuller started as a homeschooler and became a hybrid homeschooler. Her trajectory provides a good model for this book. Before getting into hybrid homeschooling, it is important to understand homeschooling. This chapter covers the basics: homeschooling's recent rise in popularity, its place within the history of education in the United States, the changing population of homeschoolers, and common challenges and concerns about the practice.

But first, we need to establish what "homeschooling" means. A great source for that is *Homeschooling in America: Capturing and Assessing the Movement*, first published in 2012 and reprinted in 2014, by Joseph Murphy of Vanderbilt University. This is perhaps the single best compendium of research on homeschooling in the United States, and much of the information from this chapter is based in the yeoman's work he did compiling and organizing the extant literature.

Murphy offers four areas for observers to consider in defining homeschooling: *funding, control, provision,* and *venue*. A true-blue homeschooled child is one whose education is funded by their parents, controlled by their parents, provided by their parents, and takes place in their home. Children who attend online schools at home, for example, are not homeschool students. Only children whose families lead all decision-making about their education are considered homeschooled.

To modern readers, this may sound radical—but it's an old concept. Homeschooling was the predominant system of educating children both in the United States and abroad for centuries—it wasn't until the mid- to late 19th century that common, state-supported schools were widely available to most children. After the advent of free public schools in the mid-1800s, family-led education at home all but died out. As recently as 1970, there were fewer than fifteen thousand homeschool students throughout the United States.[1]

Homeschooling has since come roaring back. According to the best estimates available, there were 850,000 homeschool students by 1999. That number has since doubled, to an estimated 1.7 million children. This represents more than 3 percent of all school-age children in the United States.[2]

That growth shows little sign of stopping. Each year, EdChoice conducts a nationally representative survey about education policies and practices, including several questions about homeschooling.[3] Families that homeschool consistently report high levels of satisfaction. In 2018, 86 percent of homeschool families said that they were "very" or "somewhat" satisfied with homeschooling their children. That was markedly higher than satisfaction levels of families in standalone school environments: Only 79 percent of private-school parents, 78 percent of charter-school parents, and 66 percent of traditional public-school parents answered the same way. In that same survey, one in ten respondents said that they would like to homeschool their children if money or logistics were no object. Even if all of those families would not actually homeschool, it is easy to see, if barriers were lowered, the number of homeschooled students doubling or potentially even tripling.

A LONG HISTORY

New homeschoolers would be continuing a long tradition—evidence of homeschooling dates back to at least 5000 B.C.E.[4] Throughout antiquity, a child's first education took place within the family home, with parents passing down folklore and customs to their children. In their book *Centuries of Tutoring: A History of Alternative Education in America and Western Europe*, Edward E. Gordon and Elaine H. Gordon look into the Roman household, where the "Roman mother gave her children their first education" followed by the father, who taught "writing and simple mathematics."[5] While both ancient Greece and Rome featured stand-alone schools for some older boys, wealthy families also looked to tutors to come into the home and teach their children one-on-one or in small groups. Perhaps most famously, Aristotle tutored Alexander the Great at the behest of his father, Phillip of Macedon. Historian Plutarch wrote that Alexander loved Aristotle like a second father, because "he was indebted to the one for living, and the other for living well."[6]

This home arrangement persisted throughout much of European history. Notably, Isabella of Castile, thought of as the "most vigorous and most learned princess in Europe,"[7] taught her four daughters herself in the fifteenth century. Those daughters would go on to become the queens of Portugal, the Netherlands, and England, helping to spread the knowledge accumulated during the Renaissance and advocating for the importance of a classical education throughout Europe. In Great Britain, home education remained a popular option for parents who were discontented with the harsh discipline of private schools and the poor condition of "charity schools" throughout the mid-1800s. An 1854 estimate put the total number of homeschool pupils at almost 45,000, more than the 36,000 attending private schools.[8]

Home education played a central role in the United States as well. As Milton Gaither chronicles in his magisterial *Homeschool: An American History*, in the early colonies "most learning occurred in the home, as mothers and fathers passed down values, manners, literacy, and vocational skills to their offspring."[9]

Unlike later educational efforts in the home, for the first 150 years of the American colonial experiment, fathers were at the helm of their children's education. Fathers were seen as the moral head of the household. Their duties were to eke out a living on the family farm by day and instruct children gathered in front of the family hearth by night. As fathers left the farm for the factory or better environs westward, and as the "peasant fatalism" of early colonial America gave way to beliefs in upward mobility, the work of rearing and educating children shifted to mothers.

Women taking the helm of their home and their child's education presented a paradox of sorts. As Gaither argues, on one hand, it was conservative, a "reaction against the materialism and individualism of an emerging industrial order . . . it wanted to keep women at home, children good, and the nation well-mannered and pious." At the same time, it was progressive, encouraging women to be "well informed about social problems, health and nutrition, child psychology, scientific advances relative to housekeeping, and much more."[10]

Within two generations, women's authority over their children's educations would be ceded to outside forces.

Homeschooling began to decline with the advent of the contemporary public schooling system in the late nineteenth and early twentieth centuries. Although calls for a system of public education dated back to revolutionary times, it wasn't until a critical mass of parents needed somewhere for children to go while they worked that schools started to open in force. By 1870, taxpayer-supported elementary schools had opened in every U.S. state.

But many early public-school advocates also wanted state-funded institutions to reinforce their values and beliefs. Public schools became part of an evangelical Christian united front, where the "common faith was preached uniformly in public schools, Sunday schools, the pulpit, and a host of formal and informal institutions."[11] But the tides of history and the forces of modernity chipped away at this alliance and undermined its messages: The Civil War, industrialization, immigration, materialism, and Darwinism were raising new questions, and school reformers began to worry about how these forces were battering the family.

Their response? Expand the state to save the family. As Gaither puts it,

> By the early twentieth century, government was taking a much more active role in overseeing and regulating parenthood, and it was doing so, it must be stressed, to *save* the family. Faced with large-scale breakdown of the stable two-parent family, Americans turned to their government to solve the problem. Family courts were created to deal with parental neglect, adoption, juvenile delinquency, and custody after divorce. "Manual training" programs in public schools, houses of refuge, reform schools . . . and all sorts of other institutions were modeled on the family and implemented as surrogates for those whose own families were dislocated by industrial change.[12]

But as James G. Dwyer and Shawn F. Peters argue in their book *Homeschooling: The History and Philosophy of a Controversial Practice*, there was a philosophical change at work here. Education itself emerged as a complex craft requiring particular expertise:

> Implicit in this emerging system of universal public education was not only solicitude for the welfare of children and the good of society, but also a critique of the capacity of the typical family to fully educate and academically train its children as the economy and social interactions became more complex.[13]

States' compulsory education laws, first passed in Massachusetts in 1852, and finally passed in Mississippi in 1918, greatly curtailed homeschooling throughout the country. Schools became more "professionalized," and parents divided the labor of rearing children with "experts" trained in the latest scientific methods. As Gaither describes, school became "larger, more impersonal, and further removed than it had been from home life, taking on more and more of the functions parents had historically performed."[14] Education was "expanded and formalized," with report cards replacing face-to-face conversations with parents, and the "argument was constantly made that the teacher was like a surgeon, that laypeople could not possibly understand the full complexity of expertise involved in the esoteric task of teaching."[15]

There were even efforts to outlaw private schools. In 1922, the Oregon passed the Compulsory Education Act, requiring children between the ages of eight and sixteen to attend public schools. The effort, supported by the Ku Klux Klan and the Masonic Grand Lodge of Oregon, was primarily aimed at shuttering Catholic schools, but it had the effect of closing any nonpublic school. In 1925, the United States Supreme Court ruled this law unconstitutional in *Pierce v. Society of Sisters*. Writing for the majority, Justice James C. McReynolds argued,

> The fundamental theory of liberty upon which all governments in this Union repose excludes any general power of the State to standardize its children by forcing them to accept instruction from public teachers only. The child is not the mere creature of the State; those who nurture him and direct his destiny have the right, coupled with the high duty, to recognize and prepare him for additional obligations.[16]

Efforts to curtail private schooling and homeschooling notwithstanding, by 1900 half of white children and one-third of African American children were enrolled in school.[17] By the 1970s, more than 90 percent of all school-age children were enrolled. Homeschooling was nearly extinct.

A MODERN REBIRTH

Challenges emerged to the education system in the mid-twentieth century from both the political left and right. In sociologist Mitchell Stevens's *Kingdom of Children: Culture and Controversy in the Homeschooling Movement*, the history of the modern homeschooling movement runs along two parallel tracks.[18] There were the *inclusives*, generally left-of-center, progressive parents and pedagogues who were romantic in their views toward the innate abilities and character of children, believing that schools were stifling institutions that harmed children's creativity and emotional development. Then there were the *believers*, generally right-of-center, conservative, traditionalist families who opposed the secularization of the contemporary education system and the system's efforts to remove children from their families at increasing young ages.

The inclusives trace their lineage to John Holt, who, in 1964, penned *How Children Fail*, a jeremiad against oppressive school structures that destroyed children's curiosity and natural inquisitiveness. Holt coined the term "unschooling," the practice of allowing children to direct their own learning outside the strictures of formal schooling. He published several books about children's inherent motivation to learn on their own terms, which were well received in the homeschooling movement, and, in 1977, started a magazine aimed at homeschoolers called *Growing without Schooling*.

At the same time Holt was galvanizing and incubating inclusive homeschooling on the left, Raymond and Dorothy Moore were building a homeschooling movement for the believers on the right. The Moores agreed with Holt that schools were harmful for children but for strikingly different reasons. As Stevens puts it, "Where Holt advocated children's liberation from instructional authorities of any kind, the Moores presume the legitimate authority of parents."[19] The Moores saw children as fragile and the home as the best location to safely nurture them before sending them out into the world. Because parents understand their child's needs better than any bureaucrat, and better than the child herself, they should be in control. The Moores published several important books, including *Better Late Than Early*, *School Can Wait*, *Home Grown Kids*, and *Home-Spun Schools*.

As these two visions gathered steam and supporters, another crucial source of support emerged: the Homeschool Legal Defense Association, or HSLDA. Two homeschoolers, Michael P. Farris and J. Michael Smith, founded it in 1983, as a legal operation to defend the rights of homeschooling families. In the decades since, it has grown into a grassroots network of some eighty thousand homeschool families. As of 2019, membership cost $130 and guaranteed legal counsel should authorities attempt to interfere with a family's homeschooling arrangement.

HSLDA has also grown into an important source of advocacy and information. It provides federal lobbying on behalf of homeschool families, international outreach for homeschoolers throughout the world, events and webinars, a news service for breaking homeschooling news, supports for families with children with special needs, and discounts on homeschooling products and services. By 2015, according to its tax documents, the association had grown into an organization bringing in more than $10.5 million in revenue. According to those same documents, it spent $3.9 million on litigation and legal defense of homeschoolers, $4.3 million on support services for homeschooling families, and $1.4 million on "newsletters, radio broadcasts, seminars, and homeschool resources."[20]

HSLDA's growth mirrors the growth in the homeschooling movement, and its evolution beyond simple legal defense shows the growing complexity and needs of families within that movement. That leads us some basic questions: Who homeschools their kids? How are they different from the average family? Why do they choose to take on the burden of educating their children themselves, particularly when there is a free option available?

It is difficult to get an unambiguous portrait of homeschoolers in the United States. Surveys differ in their estimates of both who homeschools and why they do it. Some of this is a definitional problem, as varying organizations define homeschooling differently. The National Center for Education Statistics (NCES) defines a child as homeschooled if that child attends traditional school less than 25 hours per week. The HSLDA sets its definition at 51 percent of a child's education, while early researchers considered children homeschooled if at least 75 percent of their education was under their family's direct supervision.[21] Surveying practices vary as well, as do response rates and how researchers and statisticians cope with missing data.

That said, in 2019 the federal government published a statistical portrait of homeschoolers, including their racial, geographic, family, and regional characteristics.[22] In *School Choice in the United States: 2019*, NCES reported that white families were most likely to homeschool, with 3.8 percent of white households homeschooling their children. Hispanic families were not far behind, with 3.5 percent homeschooling. Black families were less likely, at 1.9 percent, and Asian families were the least likely to homeschool, with only 1.4 percent of families.

The geographic spread of homeschooling perhaps paints an unsurprising picture. Rural and small-town families were the most likely to homeschool. In all, 4.4 percent of rural families and 4.3 percent of families living in small towns homeschool their children. Some 3 percent of urban families homeschool, and 2.9 percent of suburban families do as well. Homeschooling is most popular in the South, at 3.9 percent of families, and least popular in the Northeast, at 1.8 percent. In the West, 3.7 percent of families homeschool; in the Midwest, it's 2.9 percent.

The economic conditions of families might be surprising, however. While there is a perception that homeschooling is the purview of the wealthy, higher-income families are actually the least likely to homeschool. The report compares rates of homeschooling among families in three categories: those whose incomes are below the poverty line ($24,036 for a family of four at the time of the survey), within 200 percent of the poverty line, or greater than that threshold.

The data show that homeschooling is most prevalent among lower-income families living just above the poverty line. These "near-poor" families reported a homeschool rate of 4.7 percent, compared to 3.9 percent of families living below the poverty line and 2.6 percent of the higher-income or "nonpoor" families. This is perhaps explained by rates of homeschooling based on parents' labor-force participation: A whopping 7.2 percent of two-parent families in which only one parent is in the labor force homeschool their children. Only 1.7 percent of families in which both parents are in the labor force homeschool, and 1.8 percent of single-parent families in which that parent is in the workforce homeschool.

We do have some more recent state-level portraits as well. In 2019, Florida's annual homeschool enrollment report showed 97,000 students were homeschooled, up from 62,500 in 2010.[23] In North Carolina, more than 109,000 students were homeschooled in 2018–2019, up from a little less than 70,000 in 2014–2015.[24]

GROWING DIVERSITY

What motivates these families? What values inspire them to homeschool? Is homeschooling growing more in some communities than others? This brings us back to Joseph Murphy's *Homeschooling in America*, in which he reviews dozens of studies to craft as complete a portrait as possible. The key takeaway is that there are some common characteristics we can ascribe to homeschoolers, although there is variation in the magnitude of the findings. Surveys might disagree as to how much more conservative the average homeschooling family is from national norms, for example, but there is agreement that they are more conservative.

Murphy identifies eleven characteristics of homeschoolers that set them apart from the average family of school-age children in the United States. Generally speaking, they are as follows:

1. Better educated, including more likely to have advanced degrees
2. Middle income—not wealthy, but not poor
3. Led by mothers who are more likely to stay out of the labor force

4. Whiter, but there is a belief that minority homeschooling populations are both undercounted and growing (more on this later in this chapter)
5. More likely to have two parents living at home
6. More religious and more likely to be Christian
7. Younger
8. More politically conservative
9. More active in the community, including voting at higher rates
10. More suburban (in an interesting contrast to the NCES data) but not concentrated in any particular region of the country
11. Slightly larger, with more children on average

It is worth exploring long-standing racial divides in homeschooling. In the earliest years of the modern movement, white families accounted for more than 90 percent of counted homeschoolers; however, there is reason to believe that the population of homeschoolers is growing more diverse. In a 2019 research brief entitled "The Changing Landscape of Homeschooling in the United States," Aaron Hirsh of the Center for Reinventing Public Education at the University of Washington compiled recent statistics to show the growth in minority participation in homeschooling. According to Hirsh, approximately 8 percent of homeschooled students were African American, and a substantial 26 percent were Hispanic.[25] While Hirsh notes a dearth of scholarly research about the surprisingly large group of Hispanic homeschoolers, there has been a sizable amount of research on the African American homeschool experience.

In a 2000 article, researchers Susan A. McDowell, Annette R. Sanchez, and Susan S. Jones reported that African Americans frequently confronted the misperception that all homeschoolers where white Christians. They also believed that they were held to a higher level of scrutiny because of their race and were thus forced to follow a "tighter" curriculum, with less experimentation and certainly no "unschooling."[26]

Other research has focused on homeschooling by African American families as a form of protest. In 2013, Cheryl Fields-Smith and Monica Wells Kisura reported the results from interviews and focus groups of black homeschoolers in Atlanta and Washington, D.C. Many families recalled intensely negative experiences in traditional public schools, including a culture of low expectations and shameful treatment of boys, and described homeschooling as a safer option to raise their children in a more positive and supportive environment that affirmed their culture.[27] Lisa Puga built on this research in a 2019 ethnographic study of black homeschoolers in

Philadelphia. Looking at the issue from a black feminist perspective, she observed the liberative elements of homeschooling that many families frustrated with traditional school models felt.[28]

The overall motivations that drive families' decisions to homeschool are only slightly different from what these specific studies of African American families have found. Federal survey data show the most common reason is a "concern about school environment, such as safety, drugs, or negative peer pressure," selected by more than one-third of homeschooling families. Families cited their dissatisfaction with academic instruction at school and desire to provide religious instruction in second and third place, respectively. The remaining survey responses cluster together at about 5 percent of respondents: "child has special needs other than a physical or mental health problem," "desire to provide a nontraditional approach to child's education," "child has a physical or mental health problem," and "desire to provide moral instruction."[29]

Researcher June Hertzel identifies seven major motivating factors. They are as follows:

1. instructional and curricular issues
2. safety issues
3. social issues
4. convenience issues
5. health/handicap issues
6. values issues
7. self-esteem issues[30]

Other researchers have organized the various motivations differently, but the general thrust is the same. Families believe that their home is a better and more nurturing environment for children, whether that is because it is more structured than a traditional school or less structured than a traditional school. Homeschooling parents believe that they know their children better than outsiders and can do more to get the very best out of them, although the "best" might mean different things to different people.

CRITICISM AND CONCERN

Indeed, that variable definition of the "best" is at the heart of the most common objection to homeschooling. Is it in a child's best interest? How can we be sure that children are learning what they need to know?

Perhaps the best articulation of these fears comes from a 2009 article by Robin West of Georgetown Law School in the journal *Philosophy and Public Policy Quarterly* titled "The Harms of Homeschooling." West offers seven potential harms.

1. Greater risk of unreported physical abuse
2. Public health risk due to lack of immunization
3. Lack of respect for the individuality and independence of children
4. Political indoctrination
5. Reinforcing unethical, authoritarian child-rearing practices
6. Low-quality education and lack of necessary training in the basics of literacy and numeracy
7. Lack of interest in participating in the workforce on the part of parents and lack of preparation for the workforce on the part of children[31]

Some of these criticisms stem from general fears about a lack of regulation on any endeavor—that without government oversight, we run the risk of lower quality, abuse, or failure to adhere to norms. Other criticisms stem from particular assumptions about the types of people who choose to homeschool and the organizations that advocate for them, for example, that they are predominately wealthy, white, and conservative Christians.

Harvard law professor Elizabeth Bartholet raised similar concerns about homeschooling in the *Arizona Law Review* in early 2020, synthesizing several of the strands of these arguments. She argues that homeschooling "poses real dangers to children and to society." Bartholet continues,

> Children are at serious risk of losing out on opportunities to learn things that are essential for employment and for exercising meaningful choices in their future lives. They are also at serious risk for ongoing abuse and neglect in the isolated families that constitute a significant part of the homeschooling world.[32]

Christopher Lubienski raised two additional objections in an article in the *Peabody Journal of Education* in 2000. First, he argues that homeschool families are more likely to be engaged and possess the means to have a positive influence on their child's school. By opting out of school, those families can no longer serve as a resource that could potentially benefit their child's peers. Second, and relatedly, by exiting the system, homeschoolers risk hastening the decline of public schools as an institution by refusing to participate in the democratic process of overseeing schools.[33] In Lubienski's own words,

Homeschooling is both a more benign and more destructive form of privatization: benign because it does not put a claim on public resources (as do for-profit charter schools, for instance), and destructive in that it is a more fundamental form of privatization. It privatizes the means, control, and purpose of education and fragments the production of the common good not simply to the level of a locality or ethnic group, but to the atomized level of the nuclear family.[34]

Remedies for these issues vary. Dwyer and Peters devote the second half of *Homeschooling* to an argument based on the belief that children are distinct legal people with rights that must be safeguarded by the state. They argue for state oversight of homeschooling, including a "meaningful prequalification procedure and subsequent periodic assessment of the homeschooled children's academic progress and basic well-being."[35] Bartholet goes further, proposing a "presumptive ban on homeschooling, allowing an exception for parents who can satisfy a burden of justification. And it should impose significant restrictions on any homeschooling allowed under this exception."[36]

What might satisfy such a burden of justification, were it imposed? This scenario points to a major underlying question about homeschooling: Does it actually work? This is an incredibly difficult question to answer—as with any element of education, its ultimate value is evident years after the fact, after the student has completed his or her studies and put them to use in adult life. And embedded in the question is an assumption that there is agreement as to what constitutes working. What does it mean for a school to benefit a student? Is it academic? Social? Moral? And even if we agree on those things, how can we best measure them? If schools are pursuing unique or nontraditional ends, do the same metrics used to measure performance in traditional schools tell us anything?

In 2017, Brian Ray of the National Home Education Research Institute published a review of the empirical research on homeschooling in the *Journal of School Choice*. Ray compiled the available peer-reviewed empirical studies of homeschooling on academic achievement, social development, and later-life outcomes through a systematic search of the existing literature.

With respect to academic achievement, Ray identified fourteen quantitative studies. None of the studies were experimental in nature and at best can give a description of the academic skills of homeschool students compared to public-school students, adjusted for demographic characteristics. In eleven of the fourteen studies, homeschool students outperformed their peers. One study showed a mix of positive and negative effects, one showed no effect, and one showed a mix of neutral and negative effects.[37] Remember, since these are descriptive studies, we cannot conclude that homeschooling caused these differences. We can merely say there are differences in achievement.

Ray also found fifteen studies examining the social development of homeschooled children. Similar to the studies of academic achievement, these studies were descriptive, not causal, so it is important not to overstate what they found. Also like the studies of academic achievement, they overwhelmingly found positive results, with thirteen studies reporting positive findings for homeschool children and two finding a mix of positive and negative results.

Then Ray reviewed sixteen empirical studies on the long-term effects of homeschooling. These findings follow the same pattern. They looked at everything from college GPAs to political tolerance to life satisfaction. Again, these studies are not casual, they are simply describing results adjusted for differences between the homeschool and overall student population. Eleven of the studies found positive results for homeschoolers, four found no effect, and one found traditionally educated peers outperforming homeschool students.

So what can we make of all this? A couple of things. First, we are not in a place to say that homeschooling has a positive effect on the academic achievement or social development of young people. That said, we are also not in a place to say that homeschooling presents any harm to young people. In fact, the empirical literature paints a pretty clear picture that, on balance, families run little risk of academic or social harm by choosing to homeschool their children.

It would be a serious red flag if homeschooling students were, on average, performing worse academically or having worse outcomes later in life, but that doesn't seem to be the case. In fact, the opposite is true. Whether students are thriving because they were homeschooled or because of some other factors is less important. What we need to start with is this: The best evidence we have shows that homeschooling is not the risk that many of its critics seem to believe it is. And for families like Fuller's, it seems the clearest path to a bright future.

It is important to understand why some families are eager to homeschool. Schools exist in their current arrangement because the majority of families in the United States want them to look that way. It is not the imposition of an oppressive regime; rather, it is the reflection of the will of the majority.

But, in a nation as large and diverse as ours, the will of the majority will not reflect the will of all. Many minorities, be they religious, philosophical, racial, ethnic, or otherwise, do not fit into the prevailing orthodoxy. They want something different. They cannot always access it, however, because they cannot afford it or there are other logistical options standing in their way.

This is the problem that hybrid homeschooling tries to solve.

NOTES

1. Joseph Murphy, *Homeschooling in America: Capturing and Assessing the Movement*. New York: Skyhorse, 2014. Originally published in 2012.

2. K. Wang, A. Rathbun, and L. Musu, *School Choice in the United States: 2019*. Washington, D.C.: U.S. Department of Education, National Center for Education Statistics, 2019. Available at https://nces.ed.gov/pubs2019/2019106.pdf (accessed May 19, 2020)..

3. Paul DiPerna and Michael Shaw, *2018 Schooling in America Survey: Public Opinion on K–12 Education, Parent and Teacher Experiences, Accountability, and School Choice*. Indianapolis, IN: EdChoice, 2018. Available at https://www.edchoice.org/wp-content/uploads/2018/12/2018-12-Schooling-In-America-by-Paul-DiPerna-and-Michael-Shaw.pdf (accessed May 19, 2020).

4. Edward E. Gordon and Elaine H. Gordon, *Centuries of Tutoring: A History of Alternative Education in America and Western Europe*. Lanham, MD: University Press of America, 1990.

5. Gordon and Gordon, *Centuries of Tutoring*, 19.

6. Quoted in Gordon and Gordon, *Centuries of Tutoring*, 17.

7. Gordon and Gordon, *Centuries of Tutoring*, 54.

8. Gordon and Gordon, *Centuries of Tutoring*, 195.

9. Milton Gaither, *Homeschool: An American History*. New York: Palgrave Macmillan, 2008.

10. Gaither, *Homeschool*, 37.

11. Gaither, *Homeschool*, 39.

12. Gaither, *Homeschool*, 64.

13. James G. Dwyer and Shawn F. Peters, *Homeschooling: The History and Philosophy of a Controversial Practice*. Chicago: University of Chicago Press, 2019, 13.

14. Gaither, *Homeschool*, 67.

15. Gaither, *Homeschool*, 69.

16. United States Supreme Court, *Pierce v. Society of Sisters* 268 U.S. 510, 1925.

17. Thomas D. Snyder, *120 Years of American Education: A Statistical Portrait*. Washington, D.C.: U.S. Department of Education, National Center for Education Statistics, 1993. Available at https://nces.ed.gov/pubs93/93442.pdf (accessed May 19, 2020).

18. Mitchell Stevens, *Kingdom of Children: Culture and Controversy in the Homeschooling Movement*. Princeton, N.J.: Princeton University Press, 2001.

19. Stevens, *Kingdom of Children*, 40.

20. HSLDA (2015) *Return of organization exempt from income tax [Form 990].* Accessed December 2, 2020 from: https://www.causeiq.com/organizations/view_990/541719605/d0035b79255e7627b329f9a101f1af36.

21. Murphy, *Homeschooling in America*, 6.

22. Wang, Rathbun, and Musu, *School Choice in the United States: 2019.*

23. Florida Department of Education, "Home Education in Florida: 2018–19 School Year Annual Report." *Fldoe.org*, 2019, http://www.fldoe.org/core/fileparse.php/5606/urlt/Home-Ed-Annual-Report-2018-19.pdf (accessed May 19, 2020).

24. Alex Granados, "Where Are North Carolina Students Going to School?" *EdNC*, July 24, 2019, https://www.ednc.org/where-are-north-carolina-students-going-to-school/ (accessed May 19, 2020). *The Changing Landscape of Homeschooling in the United States*, Aaron Hirsh

25. Aaron Hirsh, "The Changing Landscape of Homeschooling in the United States." *Center for Reinventing Public Education*, July 2019, https://www.crpe.org/publications/changing-landscape-homeschooling-united-states (accessed May 19, 2020).

26. Susan A. McDowell, Annette R. Sanchez, and Susan S. Jones, "Participation and Perception: Looking at Homeschooling through a Multicultural Lens." *Peabody Journal of Education* 75, no. 1–2 (2000): 124–46, DOI: 10.1080/0161956X.2000.9681938.

27. Cheryl Fields-Smith and Monica Wells Kisura, "Resisting the Status Quo: The Narratives of Black Homeschoolers in Metro-Atlanta and Metro-DC." *Peabody Journal of Education* 88, no. 3 (2013): 265–83. DOI: 10.1080/0161956X.2013.796823.

28. Lisa Puga, "Homeschooling Is Our Protest: Educational Liberation for African American Homeschooling Families in Philadelphia, PA." *Peabody Journal of Education* 94, no. 3 (2019): 281–96. DOI: 10.1080/0161956X.2019.1617579.

29. Wang, Rathbun, and Musu, *School Choice in the United States: 2019.*

30. June Hertzel, "Literacy in the Homeschool Setting." In P. H. Dreyer (ed.), *Literacy: Building on What We Know*, pp. 60–81. Claremont, CA: Claremont Reading, 1997. Cited in Murphy *Homeschooling in America*.

31. Robin L. West, "The Harms of Homeschooling." *Philosophy and Public Policy Quarterly* 29, no. 3–4 (2009): 7–12.

32. Elizabeth Bartholet, "Homeschooling: Parent Rights Absolutism vs. Child Rights to Education and Protection." *Arizona Law Review* 62, no. 1 (2020): 3.

33. Christopher Lubienski, "Whither the Common Good? A Critique of Homeschooling." *Peabody Journal of Education* 75, no. 1–2 (2000): 207–32.

34. Lubienski, "Whither the Common Good?" 215.

35. Dwyer and Peters, *Homeschooling*, 226.

36. Bartholet, "Homeschooling," 57.

37. Brian D. Ray, "A Systematic Review of the Empirical Research on Selected Aspects of Homeschooling as a School Choice." *Journal of School Choice* 11, no. 4 (2017): 604–21. DOI: 10.1080/15582159.2017.1395638.

2

WHAT IS HYBRID HOMESCHOOLING?

It's June 2019, and I am getting a respite from a muggy Washington, D.C., afternoon in the study-like lobby lounge of the Tabard Inn. The Tabard Inn is supposedly the oldest operating hotel in the city, first opening its doors on N Street in 1922. It is dark, cozy, and cool in the summer, with exposed wooden beams crossing the low-slung ceiling and quirky, mismatched upholstered chairs and couches creating snug seating nooks around the room.

I'm waiting to meet Josh and Rebecca Good, who helped found the Augustine Academy in Delafield, Wisconsin. In a former life, Josh and I worked together at the American Enterprise Institute, and I knew through social media posts that he and Rebecca had something to do with a new-ish private school that had homeschooling as part of its model. I thought they might help me understand why they started a "school" that counts on parents to do some of the teaching, how this kind of operation even works, and who wanted to sign their children up.

When they arrive, Rebecca does most of the talking. A former analyst with the consulting firm McKinsey & Company, as she speaks, she winds business acumen with fervent faith. The heart of their entrepreneurial education story was one that lots of folks could relate to. They moved from Washington, D.C., to Wisconsin so Josh could take a new job and were looking for a good school for their kids. When they couldn't find one, they contemplated homeschooling, at least temporarily, until a better option emerged.

Here's where their story might veer off a bit from the typical script. The Goods had a few specifics they were looking for. They wanted a school that was rooted in their Christian understanding of the world—which itself should have been easy enough to find. But they were also smitten with a particular pedagogical model. They loved the Ambleside Method, a philosophy based on the writings of late nineteenth- and early 20th-century English educator Charlotte Mason. The method involves deep engagement with great works of literature; a rigorous approach to such disciplinary subjects as math, grammar, and languages; and a nurturing school environment that cultivates children as full human beings, ripe for habit formation and alighting of moral imagination. They'd seen such a school ten years prior, when passing through the Texas Hill Country while dating, and the sophistication of the ideas and character promoted in the classroom left such a mark that they desired it now for their own children.

Ambleside educators talk about inverting the triangle of education. Rather than seeing education as the process by which a teacher (at the top of a triangle) interprets content or data from the text (bottom corner) for the student (opposite corner), often by speaking for 75 to 80 percent of a class hour, Ambleside puts the text at the top, elevating the ideas found in great works of literature as the ultimate source of knowledge. Teachers and students work to understand texts together. Rather than the teacher running the show, it is the text itself that provides the direction, and students learn to access insight, not wait for an instructor to tell them what is worth knowing.

The problem for the Goods is that most Ambleside schools are private and expensive. And there wasn't one in Wisconsin. Charlotte Mason's methods are used by plenty of homeschoolers, however not as cohesively as they'd seen in Ambleside schools, and while the Goods wanted to be intentionally present in their children's moral and intellectual development, they valued regular peer interaction and other sources of authority for their children—and, frankly, they never saw themselves full-on homeschooling.

But then they, along with another founding couple, had a crazy idea. What if they could have it both ways? What if they opened an Ambleside school—but one that regularly involved parents as teachers some of the time? They didn't have the resources to found a traditional private school, and since their faith convictions told them parents should be active leaders in their children's formation, that wasn't necessarily the goal anyway. The Goods wanted to craft something that wasn't quite homeschooling but wasn't quite traditional school, either. They had taken part in hybrid school models in Washington, D.C., where children would only attend formal classes for part of the week and work from home the rest of the time, so they knew it could work. A hybrid homeschool could keep parents' commitments reasonable and school operating costs low. They might just be able to pull it off.

Together with their friends, the Goods gathered a group of families from their new church and budding social circle, meeting in living rooms and local libraries to pitch a novel educational idea—families could give their children an intellectually rigorous, spiritually rich education, rooted in the values they held dear at a considerably lower cost than what most private schools were charging.

It sounded impossible. But it wasn't. Families could get just what they were looking for, as long as they were willing to pitch in and lead instruction at the hybrid homeschool the Goods were proposing.

HYBRID HOMESCHOOLING, DEFINED

To get their hybrid homeschool off the ground, the Goods first had to explain what exactly a hybrid homeschool is. The simplest definition is a school that for some part of the week educates children in a traditional brick-and-mortar building and for some other part of the week has children educated at home.

But, the skeptic asks, don't all schools educate children for some part of the week in a traditional brick-and-mortar school and for other parts of the week have children educated at home? (Okay, not boarding schools. But *virtually* all.) Why are we creating a separate definition for a school where children attend formal classes on Monday, Tuesday, and Thursday, and stay home to learn on Wednesday and Friday? Is that so different from a school where children are in class five days a week, have homework and after-school activities, and go places like the local library or museum with their families on holidays and weekends?

Yes. This is not a distinction without a difference. Hybrid homeschools are a thing. Hybrid homeschooling inverts the traditional organization of schools. Rather than having the school or teacher setting the standards and expectations, and parents working with their children to meet them, parents come first here, and the school exists to support them.

Recall Joseph Murphy's framework: A homeschooled child is one whose education is funded by their parents, controlled by their parents, and provided by their parents, and takes place in their home. Hybrid homeschooled children have an education that is *partially* controlled by their parents, is *partially* provided by their parents, and takes place in the home for *part* of the school week. To qualify as a hybrid homeschool for the purpose of this book, the arrangement must meet three criteria: *physical, regular,* and *substantial.*

A student needs to go to a physical school location, at regular intervals, for a substantial amount of time—at least one school day per week. Students who spend all of their time at home but work on an online educational program prescribed by a school or through a home-study curriculum are not hybrid homeschoolers, nor are students and families who participate in homeschool co-op groups that occasionally meet for enrichment classes, field trips, or shared activities. While both cases are interesting interpretations of the homeschooling model, they are not the primary phenomenon under the microscope here.

Hybrid homeschools like the Augustine Academy, which the Goods went on to found in 2016, are. In the elementary-grade years, Augustine students attend school on-site from 8:20 a.m. until 3:45 p.m. every Monday, Tuesday, and Thursday. Wednesdays and Fridays are homeschool days, when parents facilitate at-home learning activities, including those of their own choosing, in their role as "coteacher." Older students spend just two days a week on-site and are expected to complete six hours of learning activities on each homeschooling day in partnership with their parents. Officially, the state of Wisconsin considers Augustine students as enrolled in a private school, even though homeschooling is a foundational part of its model.

That's just one way to do hybrid homeschooling. There is so much variety it can be difficult to draw strict categories for all the ways families combine learning at home and at school. According to a 2015 report by the Education Commission of the States, twenty-six U.S. states allow homeschool students to participate in activities in their local school district, from sports and extracurriculars to academic classes.[1] The line between homeschool and school can be pretty fuzzy—but it's almost always been that way.

THE HOME–SCHOOL CONNECTION

Education throughout the world and in the United States is a system that began in the home and evolved to the school. It wasn't a clean break. The transition from home-based to school-based education happened gradually, and it wasn't a one-way migration. Plenty of programs that blended home and school have persisted throughout time, leaving bread crumbs that can help us understand the hybrid homeschool models of today.

Consider "dame schools" and "cottage schools," both of which straddled the line between home and school. From the seventeenth to the nineteenth centuries, women would often agree to teach children other than their own in their kitchen or parlor for pay. These "dame schools" were used primarily to teach young pupils basic literacy, numeracy, and religion, and get them out of the house for some portion of the day so that parents could work. More recently, "cottage schools" emerged as families joined forces to offer group instruction to children in homes or church basements. They trace their roots back at least 100 years to the kinds of informal schools on the American frontier that grew up based on necessity in sparsely populated areas. They remain in many places today, with varying levels of organization and formality. Some cottage schools meet the definition of hybrid homeschooling proposed here, and some do not.

This type of informal, home-based instruction has two central challenges. The first can be broadly identified as curricular. What should students be taught and when? How can parents make sure that students are learning the things they need to know in the order that will make it comprehensible? The second is perceptual. How can we convince institutions of higher education or employers that students have learned what they need to advance to the next stage in life?

Both of these problems plagued rural and frontier families in the United States at the turn of the twentieth century. In 1905, Virgil Hillyer, the Harvard-educated headmaster of the prestigious Calvert School in Baltimore, Maryland, came up with a solution: the correspondence course.[2] Hillyer developed home-based lessons and instructional materials and mailed them to families throughout the country and the world, gaining fame and, in the next 110 years, some 600,000 students in 90 countries. Many of the resources have become digital, but the curriculum still exists today and grants accredited high school diplomas under the aegis of Calvert Homeschool.

Such correspondence-style schools and courses played a huge role in homeschooling in the twentieth century. Perhaps the best known is the Christian Liberty Academy School System (CLASS) program, launched in 1967, by Paul Lindstrom. It added an explicitly Christian element to home education correspondence courses and was the dominant player in correspondence curriculum for more than thirty years. At its peak in 1998, more than 35,000 families used it.[3]

The Clonlara school of Ann Arbor, Michigan, was also launched in 1967, and was designed to handle the administrative tasks of homeschooling so parents could focus on educating their children. Clonlara maintains homeschool students' transcripts, important records, and files of children's work at its home office, and helps parents classify their informal activities into academic subjects (e.g., bike riding as physical education and cooking as home economics). It also grants accredited private-school diplomas to these "off-campus" students who graduate from the program, in addition to those who attend its small brick-and-mortar school.[4] For the 2020–2021 school year, off-campus tuition costs $875 for a K–8 student and $1,250 for a high school student.

Correspondence schools were soon followed by homeschool support groups, which began to emerge in the 1970s and 1980s. Homeschooling families were banding together—in part because their activities were often greeted with suspicion. Milton Gaither recounts the story of Peter and Susan Perchemlides, who, in 1978, wished to homeschool their third-grade son in Amherst, Massachusetts, where Peter was a biochemist and Susan was in graduate school. Even after submitting detailed plans to the local school district, their request was denied. When their child did not report to school, the local superintendent asked for warrants for their arrest. It was only after a protracted legal battle that the family's right to homeschool their child was recognized.[5]

The impact of these groups is clear in the literature: Several such groups appear in Mitchell Stevens's *Kingdom of Children*, and Gaither describes them as a "lifeline to many struggling homeschooling mothers: providing sympathetic ears, advice for the daily grind of teaching, and especially expertise regarding how to navigate the educational and legal system."[6] Stevens writes about the Home-Oriented Unschooling Experience, or "HOUSE" group, which emerged from a group of mothers who had met through Lamaze classes and La Leche League. Inspired by John Holt, they were a more left-leaning, natural, free-spirited group that sponsored lectures and curriculum fairs, and connected homeschooling families. Stevens also documents a competing group, the Illinois Christian Home Educators, who organized to provide a network of support for more conservative, traditional homeschooling families.[7] Organizations like these have sprung up in every state in the country.

Some support groups birthed homeschooling co-ops, or arrangements between homeschooling families to collaborate on classwork, extracurricular activities, and field trips. Parents with particular expertise in science or a foreign language agreed to teach other homeschooled children. Families would coordinate trips to museums and science centers. As the numbers of homeschooling families grew, some of these small groups became more formal. In recent decades, homeschool sports teams have given rise to homeschool sports leagues. There are homeschool play productions and orchestras. There are physical locations for homeschool co-op classes. Again, the lines between home and school are blurred.

Homeschool students also participate in activities in their local public schools. This has long been the case in high school sports. Tim Tebow, one of the most talented high school and college athletes of all time, played football for Nease High School in Ponte Vedra, Florida, and led his team to a state championship even though he was homeschooled. He was allowed to do this according to a state statute, now known as the "Tim Tebow Law," that allows homeschool students who live within the attendance boundaries of public schools to participate in sports. These laws have proved controversial, with states like California explicitly banning homeschool students from playing on public-school teams.

But, as Gaither argues, most school districts tend to prefer accommodation to confrontation. In the homeschooling context, this has often meant creating programs to serve homeschoolers. According to the Education Commission of the States, "More than half of states allow homeschooled students to participate in extracurricular or cocurricular activities during or after school, attend academic classes at a local public school part-time, or both."[8]

Consider the Fleming County Schools district in Kentucky, which has sought to actively recruit homeschool students to enroll but continue to school at home under the supervision of a certified teacher. The move is empowered by state regulations that base high school credits and diplomas on demonstrated mastery rather than seat time and was inspired, at least in part, by the estimated $440,000 in funding revenues that the district did not receive in 2017–2018, due to more than one hundred local students opting to be homeschooled.[9] We'll hear more about Fleming County later. Their decision to reach rapprochement with homeschoolers rather than see them as enemies offers useful lessons for other traditional public school districts.

In the state of Vermont, homeschool students are allowed to take classes at their local public school so long as at least three of their "core academic" classes (English, math, history, and science) are conducted at home.[10] In Nevada, homeschooled students can take as many as three classes per semester at their local public school on a space-available basis, with the cost covered by the state department of education.[11]

TYPES OF HYBRID HOMESCHOOLS

Hybrid homeschools are seen in every sector of U.S. K–12 education. Figure 2.1 presents a taxonomy of the various partners that engage homeschoolers in hybrid arrangements.

Under the two broad domains of public and private schooling, there are subsequent kingdoms and phyla. Within traditional public schools, districts like Berrien Springs in Michigan directly operate such hybrid homeschool programs as its Virtual Academy Partnership, creating opportunities for homeschool students to have regular classes in a traditional school environment. Students enroll as part-time students but maintain their status as homeschoolers and can take a variety of classes, including college-level and project-based learning courses, paid for by tax dollars. This is different from more traditional part-time enrollment because the program is specifically tailored for homeschoolers. It does not simply put homeschoolers into traditional public-school classes. Such homeschool partnership programs are not new. As Patricia Lines writes in a 2000 article in the *Peabody Journal of Education*, there were examples of these programs in Alaska, California, Iowa, and Washington stretching back more than three decades.[12]

There also are district-operated or "dependent" hybrid charter schools. The Hallmark Charter School in Fresno County, California, for example, describes itself as a "partnership with parents who choose to educate their children at home."[13] Students and families complete a curriculum at home and have the option of attending classes or joining clubs on campus, for instance, robotics, advanced math, or debate. It began as a correspondence-style dropout recovery program but expanded to offer more standardized courses when school leaders realized that students needed more structure; today it has the flexibility of a charter school but is operated by the local

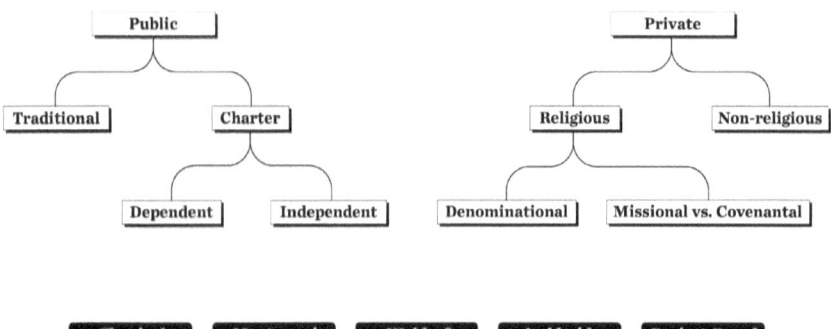

Figure 2.1. Parents' Partners: Types of Hybrid Homeschools

WHAT IS HYBRID HOMESCHOOLING? 37

school district. It shares the same board of directors as the district, and its educators are employees of the district. Such schools are often able to enroll students outside of their normal geographic catchment area and freed from many of the requirements that a traditional public school would have to follow but are deployed as supplements to a district's other offerings in coordination with the district's other schools.

There are also independent hybrid charter schools. Da Vinci Connect in Hawthorne, California, has students on campus two days per week to work through constructivist, project-based lessons and has them work from home the other three days of the week. It is state-funded and free for families to attend. Unlike Hallmark, it has its own board of directors and is an independent nonprofit organization. While these schools are occasionally authorized by school districts, they operate completely independently of them. They have their own boards of directors; their own accountability systems, as spelled out in their chartering documents; and the freedom to do what they want regardless of what the nearby traditional public schools might wish for them to do.

The private school side of the taxonomy is a bit harder to delineate. The usual divisions between secular and religious private schools, and between the different religious denominations that operate schools, can fold back in on themselves as schools also adopt specific pedagogical philosophies. There are Evangelical classical education-model schools and Catholic classical education-model schools. The family tree starts to look more like a shrub.

But there is one distinction, particularly within religious schools, that is worth exploring. It can be labeled "missional versus covenantal" or even "evangelism versus discipleship." Religious hybrid homeschools have differences in the orientation of the school's mission regarding its community: inward, or outward. Some schools view their mission as inherently inward-facing, creating a community from families that share deep-seated beliefs about religion, child-rearing, and proper educational pedagogy that differ substantially from the dominant culture. They are quite open to the fact that their school is not for everyone and will frequently be choosy about who they allow to join. They often require families to agree to a shared set of principles or be active members of particular churches to enroll their children.

Missional, or evangelical, schools are more outward-facing institutions. They see their school as part of larger mission to win more disciples for their faith or converts to their views about educational philosophy. While some have a broad faith statement that families must agree to, generally speaking they are more open to families of different religious and ideological persuasions, and see it as part of their task to introduce children to their faith and evangelize them. This distinction will become important in later chapters, when we hear parents and school leaders describe the types of communities that they hope to build in their schools and how they go about doing it.

The distinctions among these types of partnerships can be difficult to draw. Various networks refer to themselves as "university model," "conservatory," "cottage," or "tutorial" models. Added to this, homeschoolers often chafe against any use of the term outside of the traditional understanding, worrying that it will muddy the water and invite more interference into their choices.

But we must be clear, in every type of hybrid homeschooling programs parents have far more control of their child's education than they would in a traditional school. Take it from Chris Harper, the head of school at Grace Prep, the first university-model hybrid homeschool in the nation. He describes what they do as follows:

> I take a group of trained professionals and convince them that the child is better served with their parents than they're served with you right now. And, to get them to understand that we're not going to usurp the role of the parent, we're actually going to come alongside the parent, and maybe where the parent doesn't know how to do calculus, we're going to provide that. We really believe that the parent is the first government, the first shepherd, the first educator in a child's life.

This is not a typical school attitude.

HYBRID HOMESCHOOLS AT SCALE

The 2019–2020 school year was Barbara Freeman's fifty-third year in education. After thirty-three years in public education and a handful more as leader of a traditional private Christian high school in Fort Worth, Texas, she received a concerning call from her daughter. Freeman's grandchildren would no longer attend public school. They were being withdrawn and enrolled at Harper's school, Grace Prep, the local university-model private Christian school, which combines homeschooling with regular classes a few days each week and considers parents the "first educator."

At first, Freeman was concerned. She had heard of homeschooling; however, this hybrid model was new to her. But as she recalled attending sporting events where Grace Prep teams were competing, her skepticism started to ebb. On the sidelines, the students at the traditional Christian private school behaved like typical teenagers. The Grace Prep students were different: They were dressed more appropriately and behaving in ways befitting a Christian school. "The Christian schools' sidelines were very similar to what you would see in public school," said Freeman. "You saw the same types of cheerleaders, the same types of cheerleader uniforms, the same kind of music. The stands were behaving the same, the coaches were behaving the same." Grace Prep was doing something different. As her grandchildren entered the program, Freeman saw the impact of that approach in her own family. She commented,

> The first thing that I observed in addition to this, this is amazing model of education, it's an amazing model because it does give parents the gift of time, but we have structure, we have an amazing schedule that can transfer easily into a college campus. We have parents who are dedicated to being a true partner with the educators in the school. But we had qualified educators, and we had high standards, and those standards were being based on research in education.

It was the culmination of a long process to develop a private hybrid model with Christian practices as the focus.

Grace Prep was founded by a group of eight families that started sharing their homeschooling challenges in the late 1980s. Most were comfortable teaching elementary and early middle school grades, but as students got to high school, some parents grew less confident in their ability to provide higher-level mathematics and science courses. Some of them struggled to find outside teachers for more advanced subjects and were driving long distances to cobble together a program for their children. Initially called parent-based education, or PBE, it wasn't a homeschooling co-op. As Freeman put it, "They wanted higher standards, they wanted structure, they wanted continuity and consistency across grade levels, across the curriculum lines, both horizontally and vertically." The program opened in 1993, and today serves more than five hundred students.

Grace Prep met with such success that other families and educators started to take notice and wanted to create their own Grace Prep–like schools. That inspired the organizers to found NAUMS, the National Association of University-Model Schools; trademark the new name for the school model, university-model schools; and provide structure and support for other people who would like to start a similar school.

Today NAUMS, which also does business as UMSI (University Model Schools International) oversees a network of more than eighty schools.

Barbara Freeman is its CEO. NAUMS hosts webinars and board trainings, new-school workshops, and a national conference. Perhaps most importantly, it certifies university-model schools, granting a valuable internal imprimatur. It also works with accreditation agencies to give an external seal of approval for its schools. NAUMS is proud of its brand and protects it. Certification is central, Freeman argues, to ensure the model isn't watered down. She stated,

> Otherwise these schools would be just glorified versions of a homeschool co-op. So we have to have standards in place, policies and procedures, just like any other public school, if we are to survive the long term. And so we provide the credibility that these schools need with a trademark, with the certification process.

A few years after Grace Prep got off the ground in Texas, an innovative partnership cropped up between Denver-area homeschoolers and Aurora Public Schools. An open-minded principal, Dr. Thomas Synnott, worked with a group of families to create special classes for homeschoolers, and, in 1999, the Aurora school board approved the Hinkley Optional Program of Education, which later became known as HOPE (the Homeschool Options Program of Education).[14]

The program started with 20 students, but, by 2002, had grown to more than 150 students attending classes at a local church. In subsequent years, the district added more locations, expanded to serve other school districts, and grew the number of students enrolled. By 2010, 16 sites served approximately 1,900 students. Some of these sites were operated by the Options program, and others were turned over to their local school districts to operate themselves.

One of those programs was the Boulder-area APEX Homeschool Program, operated by the St. Vrain Valley School District. This year, almost eight hundred students are enrolled and attend classes on-site at least one day a week. While considered part-time public-school students, homeschooling is the foundation of the program. Kim Lancaster, APEX's program director, expresses many of the same attitudes that private-school hybrid homeschool leaders possess. According to Lancaster,

> What we seek to do as a program, our vision and our mission, is to come alongside parents who have chosen to be their students' primary educator and provide those opportunities for students and supports for parents that are hard to do at home. So, the kinds of classes that are really popular with our families are things like musical theater, choir, P.E.—things that you can't do

with one or two kids at home. Also, things like art, lab sciences, robotics that are equipment-heavy or require a special level of artistic skill that a parent may or may not feel like they have.

We're also trying to connect families. So, giving homeschool students the opportunity to have a peer group, to have other homeschool students that they know and connect with, to give them the opportunity to have some of those "normal high school experiences." Things like National Honor Society and student council and school dances and a yearbook and things like that, that kids really enjoy and those memories that they build.

We provide support and structure for the parents. We have a curriculum library where they can check out materials for their own use at home. We cannot dictate or require materials for homeschools, because the Colorado Homeschool Law prohibits that. It's a parent's responsibility and privilege to select materials, but we provide some things that they can use on a lending-library basis. So, they can check them out, use them at home, and return them when they're done.

We offer classes for students from kindergarten through twelfth grade. Everything from, like I mentioned, P.E. up to physics, trigonometry, precalculus. And then we have some options within our school district. Our high school students can connect to some really outstanding additional programming through our district's Career Development Center, which is career technical education, and through our district's Innovation Center, which is biomedical, industrial, internet, computer hardware, airline pilots, all kinds of interesting, really fascinating technical fields that kids can take coursework in. And there are concurrent enrollment programs that allow students to earn dual credits in high school and college.

What's common among the major hybrid homeschooling players is the primary focus on the home. Families drive decision-making. It is a decidedly humble approach by the schools and agencies that choose to partner with homeschool families, and an always-changing arrangement that can spark creativity and challenges, sometimes in the same day.

NOTES

1. Micah Ann Wixom, "State Homeschool Policies: A Patchwork of Provisions." *Education Commission of the States*, July 2015, https://www.ecs.org/clearinghouse/01/20/42/12042.pdf (accessed May 19, 2020).
2. Milton Gaither, *Homeschool: An American History*. New York: Palgrave Macmillan, 2008.
3. Gaither, *Homeschool*.

4. Mitchell Stevens, *Kingdom of Children: Culture and Controversy in the Homeschooling Movement*. Princeton, N.J.: Princeton University Press, 2001.

5. Gaither, *Homeschool*.

6. Gaither, *Homeschool*, 141.

7. Stevens, *Kingdom of Children*.

8. Wixom, "State Homeschool Policies."

9. "The Fleming County Schools Homeschool Action Plan." *Fleming Country Schools*, July 17, 2018, https://www.fleming.kyschools.us/userfiles/406/my%20files/fcshomeschoolactionplanfinalboardapproved07172018.pdf?id=14722 (accessed May 19, 2020).

10. Vermont Agency of Education, "Home Study Frequently Asked Questions: Public School." *Education.vermont.gov*, February 18, 2020, https://education.vermont.gov/documents/home-study-faq-public-school (accessed May 19, 2020).

11. Nevada Homeschool Network, "Frequently Asked Questions." *Nevadahomeschoolnetwork.com*, https://nevadahomeschoolnetwork.com/faq-3/ (accessed May 19, 2020).

12. Patricia M. Lines, "When Homeschoolers Go to School: A Partnership between Families and Schools." *Peabody Journal of Education* 75, no. 1–2 (2000): 159–86.

13. Hallmark Charter School, "About Hallmark Charter School." *Hallmark.sanger.k12.ca.us*, https://hallmark.sanger.k12.ca.us/about/about-hallmark (accessed May 19, 2020).

14. Denver Options Homeschooling, "History of Options Schools: Options Program History." *Denveroptions.aurorak12.org*, https://denveroptions.aurorak12.org/faq (accessed May 19, 2020).

3

FOCUS ON THE FAMILIES

When I was trying to track down parents to interview about their experiences with hybrid homeschooling, Allison Morgan, who founded the Classical Christian Conservatory of Alexandria, put me in touch with several families. After e-mailing parent Kristin Forner to set up a phone interview, the following reply popped up in my inbox: "Thank you for reaching out. I'm wondering if I might be able to call you on my way to or from the hospital one morning or evening next week. The drive is about twenty-five minutes, and it's kind of the only quiet/alone time I have these days."

We spoke in late April 2020, seven weeks into the coronavirus lockdown. Dr. Forner is an anesthesiologist and palliative care physician, and was in the middle of fighting the pandemic.

"We are not a typical homeschooling family," she said. Talk about an understatement. What she meant was that both she and her husband were educated in public schools, and neither of them were motivated by a strong desire to homeschool. "If someone told me that we would homeschool, I would have said, why?" she remarked.

They were initially drawn to the Conservatory for a simple reason. "We could afford it," Forner said. They wanted a classical, Christian education for their two elementary-age children, and other options in the Washington, D.C., suburbs were limited. But after just a short period of time, she, her husband, and their children had become enamored with the school and its hybrid model, which includes two days a week of home study.

Forner rattled off the benefits like a doctor describing the effects of a prescription or procedure. Parents have lots of quality time with their children. Her children have become best friends as they work together at home, learning conflict resolution skills and learning to share and compromise. The model allows time for creative play. And it gives her more transparency and insight into how her children are learning compared to a traditional school model. As she watches her children pretend to be English monarchs as they play around the house, for instance, she gets a window into how they are processing the world.

The model also gives her family the opportunity to teach controversial subjects on their terms. For example, when it came time to discuss human sexuality, Forner pulled out her anatomy textbook and taught her children the proper names for human body parts. She was able to speak with them in a safe place, allowing her kids to ask questions that they might feel stupid or embarrassed for asking in front of their peers. She was able to have deep conversations, even with young children, about how God created sex and why.

She loves that there is no separation between home and school. "There is very little boredom in our home," she said. As she put it, "Learning continues all day long every day of the week," and she and her children see "everything as a learning opportunity."

It's hard not to see Kristin Forner as a superhero. She works at a hospital caring for the sick and dying in the midst of a once-in-a-century pandemic three days a week and homeschools her children the other two days. There are not a lot of folks like that. But hybrid homeschooling isn't just for superheroes. Thousands of parents throughout the country use this model to create uniquely nurturing learning environments for their children.

Eric Wearne of Kennesaw State University in Georgia is the only researcher to date who has systematically surveyed hybrid homeschooling parents about their experiences. In a series of studies throughout the country, he found that hybrid homeschoolers in religious private schools tend to be mostly affluent, white, suburban, and married. "Families in those schools report placing more value on areas such as curriculum, religion, and school culture, while placing relatively little on areas such as extracurricular offerings or standardized test results," he writes.[1]

His results from surveying parents in a charter hybrid homeschool in Southern California found a slightly different group: "on average slightly more ethnically diverse, less wealthy, and less educated compared to private, religious hybrid homeschoolers, but are also more ethnically diverse, more wealthy [sic], and more educated compared to their sponsoring school district." He found that they "tend to place more value on individualized attention and the learning environment than on religion, safety, or formal academic issues when choosing a hybrid homeschool compared to their private, religious counterparts."[2]

Because each family's reasons for and experiences of hybrid homeschooling are as different as the environments they create, it is difficult to systematically classify experiences. I interviewed more than thirty parents in writing this book, both in individual conversations and group interviews.

Four major themes appeared throughout these many discussions. The phrase "the gift of time," referring to the additional time families have with their children, came up again and again. Small class sizes and individualized attention, something that the financial model of hybrid homeschooling makes possible for families who could not afford the types of schools that typically offer this, came up as well. So did the communal nature of hybrid homeschools—time and again, parents talked about the school being a collection of people making a conscious decision to "do life together" in the shared enterprise of raising their children. Finally, and perhaps most interestingly, parents and students talked about the psychological effects of hybrid homeschooling and the ways that an on-and-off model of in-person education lends itself to reducing anxiety and helping cope with students' other special needs.

These themes are admittedly impressionistic. It is my hope that these broad brushstrokes will capture the general experience of hybrid homeschoolers and resonate with the hybrid homeschoolers that read them, although they might not perfectly represent each family's experience. Given the breadth of schools being studied here, it is next to impossible to capture each of their experiences photo-realistically. As much as possible, hybrid homeschooling families will speak for themselves, and parents will be quoted at length. Some spoke and agreed to share their names, while others asked to preserve their privacy. Still others spoke during group meetings where the promise of anonymity prompted candor and self-reflection.

THE GIFT OF TIME

Each year at back-to-school time, a meme circulates on social media of children wearing brand-new backpacks and sad faces while their mothers and/or fathers flash a big smile or jump for joy. The message is simple: Kids love summer because they don't have to be in school. Parents love fall because their kids are out of their hair again.

Hybrid homeschoolers are unlikely to hit share on that one. In fact, a central motivation for many families is to spend *more* time with their children, not less. They believe that the traditional, five-day-per-week school model can alienate children from their families. They also feel that contemporary school schedules run their children into the ground, as school that starts too early transitions to afterschool activities, followed by homework that ends too late. According to a hybrid homeschooling mother in Oklahoma,

> Now I will say in his public-school, elementary school setting, there were wonderful teachers, and we had a great experience there. But I just felt at night with the homework, sometimes it's almost like another day. Your day begins then. Usually when you want to unwind in the evenings or have your family time, we still had things to do.

This type of schedule prompted questions from a mother who now participates in a charter hybrid homeschool:

> So my children were being dropped off at 8:00 a.m., being picked up at 4:30, and then coming home and doing homework until 10:00 at night. Well, that's not the way I remember my childhood. It's not the way I want my kids to remember their childhood. And I've just started thinking, "What are you doing at school all day? Why do you have this much homework when you get home from school?"

Another parent, who had also taught in traditional private and hybrid homeschools in Georgia, put the problem this way:

> I remember sitting there looking at my students and giving them a homework assignment and they were just like, "Please no, please no." And I remember registering in my brain that they woke up at the crack of dawn and went to school, then almost all of them had either sports or activities after school, and then they went home and did thirty to forty-five minutes of homework for each class that they had. And so they would usually fall asleep at 10 or 11 o'clock at night and had not had any time for a life.

A frantic pace isn't the only problem; many hybrid homeschool families also believe that when children spend long hours in school and in activities with their peers, their teachers, friends, and coaches do more to shape them as people than their parents do. According to survey research by the National Center for Education Statistics, the single most popular reason for homeschooling in general is a "concern about school environment, such as safety, drugs, or negative peer pressure."[3] Many hybrid homeschoolers feel similarly. They want to shape their children's experiences and form the people they become. They do not wish to abdicate that responsibility.

One father offered this reflection:

> You're looking at: How are we raising kids? How are we intentional with what we're doing at home? How are we intentional about being involved in their education? Not as "drop them off for eight hours a day and then hear about how their day was," but as actually invested in doing school with them. That was a game changer for us.

But these folks aren't looking for a heavy-handed, puritanical home life. Far from it. Another father described the pace of a homeschool-day morning as follows:

> We have an hour-long breakfast. We can read the Bible together a little bit and talk. It's a slower pace. It's not rushed. So, while the school day may start a little later . . . it was very fruitful for our whole family to be together, even the kids that are not in the school right now that are younger.

A mother whose children attend the Epic Charter hybrid homeschool program in Oklahoma uses the flexibility of that particular model to craft a schedule and calendar that works for her family. Epic offers several paths to study: independent digital learning with tutoring support and individual meetings with certified teachers or in-person group study and classes at its blended learning centers. Said the mother,

> My kids aren't penalized if they have a doctor's appointment at 10:00 a.m., we don't have to bring a doctor's note. It's definitely flexible. . . . My kids go four days a week. We don't ever go Fridays. My kids do Monday through Thursday, but it's because my kids are able to get their work done. I know that's not the case for everybody in every family, but my kids know that if they get their stuff done for the week that we try to do exploring Friday and go do some sort of activity. So I love the idea of that, too.

It was clear in interviews that hybrid homeschool families find great joy in spending time together. That said, full-time homeschooling was too much time at home for them. Homeschooling is a huge commitment, and one parent often has to give up working. While families might want to spend more time with their children, full-time homeschooling can be a bridge too far.

As one dad said during a spirited group interview conducted from family living rooms and kitchens via video conference during the coronavirus pandemic,

> My wife had always talked about wanting to do homeschool, but she didn't want to do it full-time. She had mentioned it to our sister-in-law, and they do homeschool full-time. She said, "I wish that there was something where I could just homeschool part-time, but not five days out of the week."

A mother in the same group concurred. She wanted to lead her children's education, but she didn't want her family to go it completely alone: "I didn't want my kids exclusively homeschooled . . . [I wanted] some community, not for the social aspects, but just for the community aspect . . . and just a little bit of a cohort with other parents. So, that was the angle we were looking for."

A third parent shared similar thoughts:

> I would say I thought about homeschooling and was drawn to it, but I didn't want to jump full-in. So, I had thought, "If there could be a school where you get the best of both worlds and I could also work part-time, that would be great." Then, a year later, the school kind of came to be. I didn't even think there could be such a thing possible. It's been great being able to work still, because I do like working.

These families see time with their children as a gift but still need some help. They want to be in control of their child's education and lead their development, but they can't do everything. They flock to, or create, hybrid models because they need other people to fill in the gaps.

INDIVIDUALIZED ATTENTION

Another driver for many hybrid homeschool families is small class sizes and the personalized attention that comes with them. Traditionally, small classes are reserved for wealthy students whose schools have enough revenue to support smaller student-to-teacher ratios. But hybrid homeschools make that available to families with a wide range of incomes.

In a traditional school setting, it is very expensive to have small classes. In both the public and private sectors, each student brings a certain amount of revenue that follows them into the classroom, either in the form of public funding or private tuition dollars. The more children per class, the more money there is to go around. The fewer children, the less money.

Hybrid homeschools are able to make the financial model of small class sizes work. To think of it in basic terms, having half of the number of students would cut the amount of revenue in half. But if students only attend class half of the time, expenditures are cut in half as well. Thus, the school comes out even.

Survey research consistently shows that parents want smaller class sizes for their children. In a 2013 survey of Georgia private-school parents by James Kelly and Benjamin Scafidi, 80.5 percent of respondents cited "smaller class sizes" as a reason for choosing their child's private school.[4] When a nationally representative sample of parents was asked to list their top three reasons for choosing their child's school as part of EdChoice's *2019 Schooling in America Survey*, 12 percent of public-school parents, 25 percent of private-school parents, 24 percent of charter-school parents, and 20 percent of homeschool parents included smaller class sizes.[5]

Parents' reasons for wanting smaller classes differ. For some hybrid homeschool parents, it's the familiarity with and close relationships between students, teachers, and families. As a mom in the Washington, D.C., area stated, "There's really no anonymity in the school. You know that so-and-so is somebody's big brother. I think there's also a culture that's just developed over time of really empowering these older kids."

Another mother in the same hybrid school said,

> I feel like I'm able to have like a little mini parent–teacher conference on average about once a week because I'll just like text, or be like, so how's it going? I feel like I get a lot of additional help from the teachers, because they know my kids so well. I think because of the small class sizes they're really, really able to get a sense of where my kiddos' strengths and weaknesses are, and they have pretty deep knowledge of their learning styles and their personalities, too. So that's been really helpful to me as a parent.

For others, it's the ability to build lessons to fit individual students' needs, rather than forcing students to follow the pace of a big group. A mom from a charter hybrid homeschool told the following story about her son and the traditional public school her family left behind:

> It just wasn't working for him. At the end of the year he was ready to quit. He just couldn't stand it anymore. He was getting really frustrated. . . . Like the year before this, he was in second grade in the public school. And he is reading

at a sixth-grade level; however, they would only allow him to do second-grade level. So he was getting bored, and he was wanting to quit school. So I called a meeting with the school and I said, "Hey, he's hating school. He's wanting to quit. He's bored. Can we give him something more to do?" And they said, "No. We can only instruct at this level." I said, "If you give it to me, I'll do it." That was a no. The teacher actually broke down and started crying, and said, "Do you know? I don't even make him come to circle time because I know he knows the stuff. He's lost in a book, and I've got twenty-seven other students to deal with."

At the hybrid charter, where activities are adjusted to meet her child's needs, "he is excelling."

"DOING LIFE TOGETHER"

During a Zoom video call with a small group of parents from a private, religious hybrid homeschool in the Midwest, an extraordinary exchange occurred. When asked what attracted them to the school, one father told the following story about an open house the school had hosted for prospective families:

> When we met some of the other families, we were looking for folks that we could kind of go through life with and who had a similar philosophy on raising kids. Meeting some of the other families, I remember coming home and telling [his wife], "Those guys are better dads than I am. They're going to be good people for us to spend time with."

Without skipping a beat, another dad chimed in, saying, "We said the same thing about you!"

The first father went on to say,

> This is mainly not so much about the schedule or what does a day look like, but the overall process. I think that doing life and school this way, it's not just about the kid growing, but it's about the parents growing as well. We find that as much as we're trying to teach them good habits, we're learning those same things. How to be intentional with our kids. Talking with other parents about what's working, what's not. It forces us to be in community and feel more vulnerable with other people. It teaches us patience. It teaches us to be more disciplined with our time and put that into practice. Our kids start calling us out on some of those same things. So, it's a whole lifestyle to sign up for. It is really rewarding, though.

In Yuval Levin's book *A Time to Build*, he argues that a "long-standing premise of the study of institutions, and indeed of sociology since its earliest days, is that, in the words of José Ortega y Gasset, "People do not come together to be together, they come together to do something together.""[6] Starting a hybrid homeschool is a way for families to do something together. They are gathered in a shared enterprise, one that takes a unique approach to child-rearing and education. This brings together like-minded people who can support and reinforce one another. They create a community, with all of the benefits that come along with that.

A mom from a hybrid homeschool in the Washington, D.C., area put it this way:

> I like to call the homeschool community a subculture. I think when you choose to do something like this, those folks have a certain level of interest in their family, a certain level of interest in their kids, in engaging their kids. . . . In that community they're going to be the folks that are going to be like, "Oh my gosh, I guess that we're all in this together." And so I think that the folks that choose this life in its various components—whether it's full homeschool or hybrid, whatever—that in itself is a self-selected group . . . I feel like you kind of know what everyone's going through, and we all are just like, "Yes," I know she's got something going on or he's got something going on, how can I help?

She went on to say,

> And that goes through the school stuff, but it's also when a family has a child with an illness, a parent in the house has an illness, they're coordinating pickup. Or I know when I first got here, this is our first year and it was, some folks are meeting down at the water, I'm sure they'll be happy to just meet you and kind of get you into the family. And so by the time I got there in the fall I had a community already, I felt already warmly welcomed and like I could ask these questions amongst them. And so I think it's not just education that we do together, we do life together.

There is strength in community. When a member of a community needs help, there are other people there to help them. In hybrid homeschooling communities, parents know what other parents are going through. They are facing many of the same challenges. They also share beliefs about the role that families and communities are supposed to play, so they back up one another and can lean on one another when times are tough.

At the same time, most parents agree that these schools are not for everyone. It takes a certain kind of family to want to do life this way. It takes certain beliefs to want to take the lead in providing a child's education. It takes time, effort, and persistence to maintain relationships with teachers and other families. Many of these families are wary about who they choose to allow to join the communities they've created together.

Even though these hybrid schools are new, there is a conservatism to them. It was British philosopher Sir Roger Scruton who opined, "Conservatism starts from a sentiment that all mature people can readily share: the sentiment that good things are easily destroyed but not easily created."[7] It is clear that many families realize that they have built a good thing, and that allowing families in who don't share the same philosophies can destroy it. Some might see this as exclusionary. They would be right. But it is exclusion in the service of creating a philosophically coherent institution and community of mutual support.

MENTAL HEALTH

Millions of parents throughout the country struggle to find the best learning environment for their child with special needs. The "special needs" classification covers conditions that are temporary and permanent, physical and mental, emotional and social, and every combination in between. Students with special needs have unique strengths and challenges, and schools of all stripes struggle mightily to tailor the best interventions so that these students can thrive.

According to a 2016 federal survey of families of school-age children throughout the United States, 34 percent of homeschoolers attribute their decision to homeschool to their child having special needs. Some 14 percent cite a physical or mental health problem, and 20 percent cite another special need.[8]

For many families, hybrid homeschooling was an important tool to help their children manage stress and anxiety. Not all children are best suited to spend their days in loud, busy, socially demanding settings like traditional schools, and reducing the number of classroom hours helped them focus on their studies and thrive.

Numerous parents spoke movingly about their children with special needs and how a hybrid environment worked for them. One mother spoke of her son, who had bounced between different programs before finding a hybrid homeschool that worked well for him. She related,

> My son had sensory integration disorder because he was a premature baby, and so sitting in a seat in kindergarten was actually not a choice. It was just too

much for my sensory kiddo, who needed to be running around. He needed input. So [school] three days a week was the best of both worlds because he never had to go back tomorrow. If you had a bad day at school, you never had to go back tomorrow. He would say, "Mom, can I go swing on the swing and read my book?" I'm like, "Yeah, sure. Yeah. Go ahead." As a sensory kid, that input made it easier for him to comprehend. He would read in the car. [School] just ended up being a very safe place for us to help him.

Now it is also true that many hybrid homeschools cannot offer the same suite of services that a traditional public school or specialized private school can. Nor can they provide services for students who need therapies or other interventions every day. But they can supplement the efforts of parents who are taking the lead in their child's instruction.

In October 2017, *New York Times Magazine* published "Why Are More American Teenagers Than Ever Suffering from Severe Anxiety?" an in-depth investigation of the rising prevalence of anxiety disorders in young people in the United States. The article follows several young people and the organizations that help them. The statistics it cites are sobering. Anxiety is now the number-one mental health issue of college students seeking counseling services. The number of students reporting "overwhelming anxiety" in the previous year grew from 50 percent in 2011 to 62 percent in 2016.[9]

Consider the annual pulse-check by the University of California, Los Angeles (UCLA), cited in the article. For more than thirty years, as part of an introductory survey, UCLA has asked incoming freshman if they have felt overwhelmed by everything they have to do. In 1985, 18 percent of students said they felt overwhelmed. In 2016, about 41 percent of students said they felt overwhelmed. Psychologists point to everything from helicopter parents to the pressures of social media as the cause, but the result is clear: A significant portion of American students are suffering from anxiety issues.

The unique, customizable schedules powered by hybrid homeschooling can help students prevent, manage, or stave off anxiety. Hybrid schedules give students time to recharge and reset themselves before having to go back into the classroom. If they have a bad day, they can take a day off to regroup. By design, assignments can be completed at home or at school. So, if a student needs to take a mental health day, they don't lose instructional time; instead, they just work from home. These structures conspire to alleviate pressure on young people. They have time to get done what they need to get done. They have release valves that they can open when school or life gets to be too much. And, perhaps most importantly, they have closer relationships with their parents and family, who can support them as they work through their mental health challenges. They are intentionally connected to other adults in their life who are on the same page as their parents and can help share that burden.

Numerous parents confirmed this in interviews. A representative response came from a mother from Oklahoma who spoke passionately about her daughter's struggles with anxiety and how the flexibility and small, personal nature of her new school environment has helped calm it:

> I should say, my youngest daughter deals quite a bit with generalized anxiety disorder. At traditional public school, my sweet neighbor is a teacher, and she would tell me that she would go check on her at lunch and she's not eating, she's crying. Well I was never hearing any of this unless she would let me know. And it was a lot of anxiety just for everybody, because we had a little one in the house who was upset and scared all the time, and hated going to school. It has changed drastically because if she's having a day like that, which thank goodness went away very quickly, the teacher will simply text me and be like, "She's having a real rough day. Why don't you try to pick them up at lunch if you're able to." I would have never got that sort of attention . . . I have appreciated it so much. In fact, she hasn't even had to go to counseling in, I don't know, six months.

Hybrid homeschools put students and parents in greater control of learning, allowing them to find rhythms that work best for them. They are no longer chained to the Carnegie Unit (more about this in chapter 5). On homeschool days, students will frequently only have to work for as long as they need to get their work done.

Circulating through the lunchroom during a visit to a hybrid homeschool in suburban Kansas City, a group of six freshman boys and one eighth-grade boy described what their days look like when they study at home. The maturity of their answers was surprising, although perhaps it shouldn't have been. Some mentioned that they liked to start earlier in the morning, and some liked starting later. Others had to go with their parents as they dropped off siblings at school or daycare so they were limited in when they could start. But in general, they said that they could get their work done in about half the time of a traditional school day if they stayed focused and worked hard. They had internalized that hard, diligent work pays off.

These teenage boys saw the school to be more organized and less chaotic than the schools they had previously attended. But their favorite thing was the freedom that the hybrid gave them to set their own schedules at home.

Compared to their friends at other schools, they saw themselves progressing through their studies much more quickly and accomplishing far more.

Bouncing to another table of seventh-grade girls, they said they liked spending more time with their families. They also liked that on homeschool days, they "get a chance to miss their friends," as one young woman put it. They said that the school was "more relaxed," and one girl mentioned that she takes piano lessons and plays three sports, so it was "great to have time to do nothing." One young woman said that even with the reduced in-school schedule, she was learning more than she did when she was just doing school at home. Another mentioned that she was able to make more friends at the school than she had before. Several said that they simply preferred going to school on a part-time basis, although they did think that their homes have a lot of distractions that can tempt them away from their assignments.

These sentiments were echoed by parents. One hybrid homeschool mother, a former teacher in a traditional school, described it as follows:

> So I know this frustration both from my own perspective and the perspective of the students that I had. There are kids working quickly, and it's like, well it doesn't matter how quickly you work through this. This class is fifty minutes long, and it's going to meet every day. Whereas with our kids it's like, "Look, if you're diligent and you do the work that you need to do, on Fridays, you don't have to go to school and we can go exploring somewhere." That is a huge motivator for them. At traditional public school, you had to be there whether or not you were done or whether or not you understood the lesson. . . . My kids work hard because I've dangled the carrot that says, "Look, you have schoolwork Monday through Thursday. You're going to be there. So get it done." And they have really become self-motivated. Last year, because they worked ahead, they were done with the curriculum mid-April.

Hybrid homeschools take students' time seriously. They are humane institutions. By getting the most out of the time that students spend in class and giving them the freedom to do what they wish once they have finished their out-of-school work, these schools are telling students that they are engaged in something important and are active participants in their education. Wasting time in school sends a message to students that what they are doing is not serious. When classrooms are interrupted by needless announcements or days are disrupted by pointless assemblies, students see that their education is not coming first.

With limited and focused time together, hybrid homeschools can filter out these types of distractions and offer subtle cues that imbue an entire school community with a sense of calm and purposefulness. This permeates all of the school's activities both inside and outside of the classroom. It is a healthier environment for student learning.

NOTES

1. Eric Wearne, "A Survey of Families in a Charter Hybrid Homeschool." *Peabody Journal of Education* 94, no. 3 (2019): 300.
2. Wearne, "A Survey of Families in a Charter Hybrid Homeschool," 297.
3. K. Wang, A. Rathbun, and L. Musu, *School Choice in the United States: 2019.* Washington, D.C.: U.S. Department of Education, National Center for Education Statistics, 2019. Available at https://nces.ed.gov/pubs2019/2019106.pdf (accessed May 19, 2020).
4. James P. Kelly and Benjamin Scafidi, "More Than Scores: An Analysis of Why and How Parents Choose Private Schools." *Friedman Foundation for Educational Choice*, November 2013, https://www.edchoice.org/wp-content/uploads/2015/07/More-Than-Scores.pdf (accessed May 19, 2020).
5. Paul DiPerna, Andrew D. Catt, and Michael Shaw. *2019 Schooling in America Survey: Public Opinion on K–12 Education, Busing, Technology, and School Choice.* Indianapolis, IN: EdChoice, 2019. Available at https://www.edchoice.org/wp-content/uploads/2019/10/2019-9-Schooling-in-America-by-Paul-Diperna-Andrew-Catt-and-Michael-Shaw-1.pdf (accessed October 20, 2020).
6. Yuval Levin, *A Time to Build*. New York: Basic Books, 2020, 155.
7. Roger Scruton, *How to Be a Conservative*. London: Bloomsbury, 2014, viii.
8. M. McQuiggan and M. Megra, "Parent and Family Involvement in Education: Results from the National Household Education Surveys Program of 2016." Washington, D.C.: U.S. Department of Education, National Center for Education Statistics, 2017. Available at https://nces.ed.gov/pubs2017/2017102.pdf (accessed June 22, 2020).
9. Benoit Denizet-Lewis, "Why Are More American Teenagers Than Ever Suffering from Severe Anxiety?" *New York Times Magazine*, October 11, 2017, https://www.nytimes.com/2017/10/11/magazine/why-are-more-american-teenagers-than-ever-suffering-from-severe-anxiety.html (accessed May 19, 2020).

4

TEACHING IN A HYBRID MODEL

In the mid-1960s, more than 5 million U.S. schoolchildren attended one of more than thirteen thousand Catholic schools. At that time, Catholic schools enrolled 12 percent of the nation's schoolchildren. In cities like New York, more than one-third of all students attended Catholic schools.[1] But enrollment started a steep decline in the 1970s, and it has continued to drop in the decades since. From 2010 to 2020 alone, nearly 1,000 Catholic schools closed, and student enrollment dropped by 18 percent.[2] Today, the sixty-one hundred remaining Catholic schools educate 1.7 million students throughout the United States.

St. Louis, Missouri, as the name might suggest, has a deep connection to the Catholic faith. Even today, it remains dense with Catholic schools—there are more than one hundred elementary and two dozen high schools, both parochial and independent. It is also a city of hyper-local culture and tradition. Typically, one of the first questions a St. Louisan asks a new acquaintance is, "Where did you go to high school?" The answer will reveal where he or she grew up, how much money their parents had, and a host of other in-group and out-group designations known only to those steeped in the peculiarities of the city.

This would not be the first location to expect a new, Catholic hybrid homeschool to launch. And yet, in the fall of 2009, a group of parents and teachers launched St. John Paul II Preparatory School with seven students in a borrowed pole barn. It offered a classical education, called on parents to serve as "coeducators," and attracted new families by the dozen in the next few years. As it grew, it moved seven times—including, at one point, to rented space in an Evangelical church where teachers had to take the crucifixes off the wall at the end of the school day on Fridays. Today, St. John Paul II rents part of a formerly closed Catholic school and educates 160 students.

Principal Lynette Schmitz, who had spent her career teaching in local traditional Catholic schools, describes herself as a "total convert to the hybrid model," adding, "I wish that it had been available to me when my kids were young."

As it turns out, the robust and competitive Catholic high school system in St. Louis created a need for a preparatory school with a different model. Schmitz commented,

> There are lots of Catholic schools in St. Louis, really excellent Catholic schools. So there's a lot of competition out there. But what ends up happening is that, especially in the grade school, middle schools primarily, of the schools that I was at previously, they were feeding into high-level schools. And you'd find that in even fifth, sixth, and especially seventh and eighth grade, kids were doing tons of homework at night. . . . And so what we have tried to do is take the evening homework piece completely out. The idea here is that we're trying to give time back to the parents in the evening, where they can do family things, pray a family rosary, play board games, just sit and talk to Dad, or take music lessons or whatever. We're trying to give that time back so that you can cement the family bond.

The school follows a hybrid schedule, with students attending classes on campus for three days per week and working from home for two days. This brings down the price of tuition to less than one-third of the average local Catholic-school tuition, which particularly benefits large Catholic families. As Schmitz sees it,

> One of the founding principles is to be able to provide a quality, authentic Catholic education for a very reasonable price. For our families, the average number of siblings in the family is 5.2. And so the idea here is that these Catholic families, some large Catholic families, can receive a faithful, quality Catholic education for their children without having to go into extreme debt. Our high school tuition is $5,000 a year.

When asked about the types of families that attend the school, Schmitz said,

We're looking for people who are somewhat like-minded, who are interested in forming this bond with their family, deepening their faith. That's not to say that we don't have non-Catholic students. But in general, the discernment process between them and us is that a lot of times we'll have people come in, they hear about us and like the idea of the classical education. They like the idea of a somewhat traditional approach. And maybe their student has had some difficulty at some other school, so they want to investigate us. So the thing, the discernment process is, "Is this really going to be a good fit for you? Are you going to be happy here?" Because if your Catholic faith is not a pretty significant part of your life, you might find it a little overbearing in some ways.

This echoes the sentiments of many other hybrid homeschooling educators. They are meeting the specific needs of families with a unique model. That model relies on families selecting the particular school community that best fits them and schools clearly articulating their vision and expectations.

Hybrid homeschooling partnerships need to start from a place of common understanding. How do hybrid homeschools build and maintain school–family relationships? How do teachers and school leaders work with families to purposefully share an intimate educational bond? How do schools create strong communities to keep everyone moving in the same direction? What do they see as their mission? And what challenges do they face? As we'll see, different schools have come up with different answers.

CREATING A COMMUNITY

Chapter 3 details what drives parents to choose hybrid homeschools. What drives educators to get involved? The first answer is that many educators see the same problems in the education system that parents do. They don't like seeing burned-out students. They want to be part of a community where the adults reinforce, not undermine, one another. And they often have connections to a particular pedagogical philosophy or religious ethos that guides a hybrid homeschool. In different combinations, these factors inspire educators to intentionally join educational communities in partnership with parents.

Willyn Webb is executive director of Vision Charter Academy, a public charter school that offers homeschool support and individualized, part-time classes at three campuses in rural western Colorado. Webb is a former school counselor and homeschool parent who was drawn to hybrid homeschooling because it better aligned with her philosophy of how education should work. Vision's mission statement, for example, prioritizes student-centered learning, self-efficacy, compassion, and mutual respect. Webb noted,

> Well, I've been a school counselor, I've been a private therapist in the community while I was raising my own kids. I homeschooled my own kids a little bit, and then I was a counselor [at] an alternative high school. My thing all along has been individualized learning. And when this position came open, I wanted to do more with individualized learning than what I was able to do under the district umbrella at the alternative school. I think it's the way education needs to go for everyone across the country. I had written a book with a lady from Newark that was very into this, and it just really set all of my philosophical beliefs. And so I took the leap. And I had people with the district tell me I went over to the dark side. But I very readily went over to the dark side. I have enjoyed being here and doing this work . . . I mean, there are so many great twenty-first-century skills traditional schools are trying get going that are inherent in our model already.

Jennifer Cauzza, executive director of the Julian Charter School network in Southern California, had a similar story:

> My philosophy was always, we did one-on-one reading on the couch with a student. It wasn't necessarily basal readers, and I did individual spelling lists and I had six math groups. That was pretty much the way I taught in a classroom, to try and personalize individualized learning. So when I read about this and with the friction that was going on in my traditional school, I thought, it doesn't hurt to apply.

Educators in private hybrid homeschools are often drawn to them because of their religious ethos. They see the advantages of both the hybrid model and the ability to teach in schools that align with their personal religious beliefs. Martha Herndon, the head of school at the faith-based Capitol Hill Learning Group in Washington, D.C., had this to say about how the hybrid homeschooling model reinforces the religious ethos of the school:

> It really brings together the best of both models. It gives that social outlet, it provides a place that's away from home, where students are able to be in their own space, not completely influenced by family but yet still getting good modeling and positive role models. For us, the Christian worldview is still brought to them by the teachers and staff, but it gives them a place to develop on their own and to individuate a little bit from their family. At the same time, it keeps

them grounded with their family. Giving them more time than a traditional schooling student would have, to still stay connected with family.

Numerous teachers in religious hybrid homeschools valorized the homeschooling portion of the school week as an opportunity for parents to take on teaching controversial or fraught topics, for instance, human sexuality. Rather than tackling questions of morals and values in class, schools allow parents to cover that at home. It takes a weight off teachers, who don't have to try and facilitate those difficult conversations. And it ensures that teachers and families don't get crossways with one another, with the teacher teaching one thing and the parents teaching another.

But teachers also believe that the model is best for academic development. They support sharing the responsibility of education with parents, which many see as honoring the full personhood of each student and creating a more dynamic environment for learning. A teacher at Capitol Hill Learning Group put it this way:

> It's really the partnership you have with parents and the students. For me, it's the fact that this model teaches children to take responsibility for their own learning, independence in learning, which is a skill. . . . In a lot of schools, it's just about the message. It's about conforming. Here we do a lot of talking. In the middle school it's teaching such independence. It's teaching confidence. It's seeing children just coming alive to the subject material, seeing children coming alive to being able to know who they are and being independent learners and thinkers rather than just saying what you want them to. They will challenge. They will talk. We have lots of open discussions.

As described in chapter 2, there is an important distinction between the two major types of private religious hybrid homeschools: "missional" (or "evangelical") and "covenantal" (or "discipleship"). Missional schools see their purpose as evangelical. They want to attract nonbelievers to their schools to try and use those institutions to bring more souls into the fold of their faith. They cast a wide net and are comfortable with unorthodoxy in their community. While they frequently have a faith statement that the school aligns its instruction with, families do not have to adhere to it in their private lives.

Christy Wilson, dean of academics at Alliance Christian Academy in Fort Worth, Texas, describes it as follows:

> We are evangelical at our preschool. So our babies through three-year-olds, which we have a very small group. But our babies through 3-year-olds, any-

body can come. We feel like there's value in supporting young families, in sowing seeds in those young kids early. And whatever happens after that point, we plant the seed and somebody else gets to water it; however, when we get to the academy, then we have a very, I hate to say stringent, but we are discipleship. And we feel like you have to have one family member who is currently a believer. You have to be involved in a church, because we are not the church. And we want you to have resources beyond us. We'll point you to resources, but we want you to have resources beyond us.

If missional schools go wide, covenantal schools go deep. Rather than looking to recruit families who think differently, covenantal schools see their mission as creating a safe and nurturing environment for a community of families who share the same views and values. Oftentimes, they require parents to sign on to the school's faith statement to affirm that they share it. They expect parents to regularly attend an aligned church and will ask for references from their pastor.

Allison Morgan, who founded the Classical Christian Conservatory of Alexandria, summed up the covenantal mindset well when she said,

> We didn't have much of a statement of faith or an application process the first year because it was all just the founding families who were like, "Yeah, this is awesome." But we learned real quick that that doesn't work. You need to be definitive. And so we are. Our application states, not only do you have to agree to our statement of faith, you have to be a member of a local church with the pastor's name as a reference. And so you really have to live out what you're claiming is your statement of faith. You have to be in community. How can I expect you to answer to our authority as a school if you can't commit to the authority of the church? If you're not actually teaching your children any of this outside, we can't do that for you in eighteen hours a week. It needs to be in your DNA as a Christian family . . . I don't know how I talk to a parent about discipline if they're not reading the same Bible I am. That gets really muddy to me, and I just shoot myself in the foot.

Many families in covenantal schools see them as a refuge from a culture that is at odds with their values, both in education and the wider world. It shouldn't surprise us that they want to control who they allow into that refuge.

Covenantal or not, most hybrid homeschools try to be clear with parents that they are doing something unique and that parents should know what they are getting into. It is quite common to hear educators explicitly say, "This school isn't for everyone." They work to inform parents during school visits and open houses as to how the school operates and push families to think about whether the school is a good fit. Lynette Schmitz of John Paul II Preparatory described the motivation as follows:

> The idea is, "Here's who we are. Do we fit with what you want for your family?" And it's not so much us saying, "No, I don't think you're going to fit here." It's more, "This is who we are, and we're not necessarily the place for everyone, but will we fit with what you want for your family?"

That said, schools generally rely on standard mechanisms to attract new families, for example, open houses, social media, and word of mouth. Once families have agreed to join the community, many schools offer a parent boot camp before school starts to get them up to speed on being a coteacher. Belinda Henson, head of the school at the Legacy Classical Christian Academy in Fort Worth, Texas, described the process, saying the following:

> We have parent-driven professional development; we call it coteacher college. So for the first week of school our parents are learning about the curriculum, learning how do you score a math homework sheet, what does a math meeting look like in class, how do you help your child write a paper? So we provide them with some skills at the beginning of the year in hopes of helping them throughout the year.

Attracting the right parents and getting them up to speed is half of the battle. The rest relies on great teachers.

TEACHERS

Since Horace Mann opened the first "normal" school in 1839, in Lexington, Massachusetts, for the state-supported preparation of teachers, the professionalization of the teaching force has been a key effort of education reformers. Debate has raged about how teachers should be prepared, how they should be licensed, how they should be compensated, how they should be evaluated, and more. Should teachers have to pass a licensing test to be able to teach? Should student test scores be used to evaluate them? Should they have tenure?

Why all the fuss? Well, research has repeatedly shown that teachers are quite important—a revelation that should surprise no one. Good schools need good teachers, and hybrid homeschools are no exception. These schools present unique challenges for career educators, however. First, teaching in a hybrid environment is fundamentally different from teaching in a traditional school. Teachers have to buy into a philosophy that does not put them at the center of a child's instruction. They also have to be willing to adjust their pedagogy to support home learning and fit the schedule of the school, as well as the types of students that they will be serving. It takes a special type of teacher to thrive.

School leaders identified a few major challenges for teachers taking on a hybrid homeschooling role. Students' expectations for classroom behavior and rules are different, as are parents' expectations for their active role in leading and grading assignments. That is part of the dynamic at the Summit Academy in suburban Denver, according to Tim Matlick, the executive director. Said Matlick,

> We hire a lot of traditional teachers that want to teach in the homeschool, but it is actually really different to train them because classroom management is completely different. These kids learn differently. They are actually taught at home to tune out a parent's instruction unless their name is given first. So, in a traditional setting you're like, "Everybody turn to page 12." At the homeschool setting it would be, "Steve, turn to page 12." And unless they hear their name first, they tune it out completely. So yeah, there's a lot of understanding that needs to be built with traditional teachers that this classroom is going to look different. . . . They're actually really well behaved, but they have so much flexibility when they're doing their work that they're not accustomed to group instructions and group work. And so, if you give an assignment to the homeschool kids, they're going to do it twelve different ways. And so trying to corral them into doing it potentially one way, that's where it takes a little bit more of the effort. But they're actually great kids. They're not defiant, they're not disruptive. They're just really happy doing their own thing. That's where the managing comes in.

Belinda Henson of Legacy Classical Christian Academy was explicit about the challenges. She related,

> If we have a teacher who comes to us who has been teaching for fifteen or twenty years and they're not used to a parent e-mailing them and saying, "I don't understand this assignment, explain it to me," and the teacher's attitude is, "Well, I already told your child how to do it, I don't need to tell you also," that doesn't work because you're really in partnership. They're a coteacher.

In addition, many hybrid homeschools layer a pedagogical philosophy or religious ethos on top of the hybrid schedule, compounding the demands on teachers. Christy Wilson outlined the issue well, stating,

A lot of our teachers are former teachers who stayed home with their kiddos when they were little. [They] found us because they taught in public schools, they wanted something different for their own kids, but they didn't necessarily want to do it on their own. . . . It is a different model. First off, we're classical, which throws public-school teachers for a loop. And second of all, it's a different model. So we tell them, "Listen, we've been doing this long enough, it's going to take you at least a semester of saying, 'I don't get it, I want to get it, I want to do this in the classroom.'" And we're like, nope. That goes home to parents, you don't do that in the classroom, this is what parents do. No, you don't check that, a parent checks that. You use your classroom time for this. Usually about January of their first year they're like, "I get it, it finally clicked."

WORKPLACE TRADE-OFFS

Teachers may ultimately like working in hybrid programs, but as currently constituted, it is difficult for many private hybrid homeschools to attract traditional candidates for teaching. In general, teachers earn only a fraction of what traditional public- or private-school teachers are paid. Hybrid homeschool teachers make a trade-off; they forgo pay but gain a more flexible schedule in a more supportive community. This works for many retired teachers who are already drawing a pension and wish to keep working on a part-time basis or supplement their income, or for married teachers whose families can afford to have one spouse working part-time, or for teachers that can find another source of income to supplement their salary.

Ron Lawlor, principal at Christ Prep Academy in Kansas, noted that hybrid homeschool teachers are usually working just three-fifths of a full-time job. "The question is," he asked, "how many people can live on three-fifths?" Here is how he says they are trying to tackle the problem:

> The biggest challenge we have is finding younger teachers who can afford to come in. . . . We have a terrific new young teacher who is with us on Tuesday and Thursday. She makes it, because she subs on Monday, Wednesday, and Friday in one of the local districts. And they discovered right away what we discovered, that she's going to be a great teacher. So they call her all the time. So the fact that she subs Monday, Wednesday, Friday and then is with us on Tuesday, Thursday makes it much more manageable for her.

Public hybrid homeschools may have a leg up in addressing this challenge. Lynn Pollitt is executive director of the Mountain Phoenix Community

School, a Waldorf-model public charter school in suburban Denver that offers a hybrid homeschool program and traditional, five-day-per-week school option. That school has teachers that bounce back and forth between traditional and hybrid instruction. That fills teachers' schedules, and they enjoy the change of pace, she said. Pollitt added,

> Most of them are already Waldorf teachers or they have been classroom assistants, and so they have been trained and are working through that.... They may come over and teach homeschool for an hour or two, and then they go back to their regular classroom schedule.... A lot of teachers are asking to come to the homeschool program, because they really enjoy working with these kids, and it's kind of a nice break from their five-day-a-week classroom. Now everybody wants to be in homeschool.

Compensation challenges notwithstanding, many teachers see value in the model, both in the way that families and educators work together and the flexibility that it offers. A D.C.-area teacher who taught for more than ten years in public schools and then homeschooled for twenty years made this comparison during an energetic group interview:

> It's a model set up for success because the parents have to be involved. At other schools, they try to get parents involved, but PTA work isn't the same kind of parent involvement as a hybrid school. It's just not the same.... When I was in the public school, I didn't get a lot of parent involvement. A lot of times when you saw parents, it was at a meeting with all of the teachers, because the student was in big trouble academically or behavior-wise. And so you didn't really see parents, you didn't really, maybe once a year at a parent conference or something. But not like this. We have sometimes daily contact with parents now. So I'm a lot involved with the families, not just the students. I know the whole family.

A teacher from another hybrid homeschool in the D.C. area also noted that the shorter school day allowed her to work while still spending time raising her two young sons. She said,

> Before, I was working from 7:00 a.m. to 3:00 p.m. That was the day. That was the set day. Here it's 9:00 a.m. to 1:00 p.m. I'm naturally a morning person, but 9:00, to me, is late. I wake up naturally before going to work, which is very odd. I wake up naturally. I have that time in the morning to spend with God, still spend with my kids, make breakfast if my kids are up at that time, and still be with my family. I can teach for those few hours and still come home, write a little bit before nap time, and still catch my kids. Being a mom of two young

> boys—I have a six-month-old and an almost three-year-old—I value family. For me, it was either this or nothing. If I wouldn't have found a model like this, I would still be a stay-at-home mom.

That's not a universal experience, however, another teacher in the same group interview responded.

> I think that also depends on the role that you're playing within the school, because I can't vouch for having much time at the moment. I'll be very honest with you, as heading up the middle school and also teaching language arts, I teach three classes, three subjects, that's nine sets of prep, as well as overseeing the parents and the school, the children, I work a full day almost every day.

Belief in the mission of the school is a large driver of teachers willing to make sacrifices to teach there. Many teachers working in traditional environments are motivated by a similar sense of mission and commitment to their students, schools, and communities. But in hybrid homeschools, where the "school" can shift shape day to day, the compensation and benefits are unlikely to approach those in a typical school, and teachers share control with parents, the mission must pull much harder.

A HYBRID CLASSROOM

Vision and mission aside, a straightforward question remains: What is it like to teach in a hybrid homeschool? Shadowing two eleventh-grade girls during their advanced algebra and British literature classes at a hybrid homeschool in suburban Kansas City helped answer that question. That day, the algebra class was working through arithmetic sequences, finite and infinite geometric sequences, and the binomial theorem. The thirteen students sat at a hodgepodge of tables and chairs that had clearly been used for something else before. The room was spartan, with a podium and large whiteboard at the front. Even though it was a Christian school, the class did not start with a prayer, and while there was a Bible in the corner of the room and a "Pray for the Persecuted" poster on the bulletin board, there was no other outward indication of the school's religious ethos.

The class was relaxed, the students were attentive and well behaved, and the rapport between them and their teacher was caring and kind. When the teacher made a mistake in working through a sample problem, the students corrected him and everyone laughed about it. The pedagogy was pretty old-school: The teacher provided direct instruction on the concept, worked through several examples on the whiteboard himself, and then called on individual students to solve additional problems on the board. The class ended with a homework check, and the students were out the door.

Chatting briefly with the teacher after class, he revealed that he had taught at schools throughout the world and was taken by the hybrid homeschooling model because "full-time schools waste a lot of time." When asked about adaptations he has had to make, he responded that he didn't really need to adjust his methods. His planning is a bit different, and he gives kids more homework because they have more time to do it. That said, he used a standard textbook and would finish the school year at the same endpoint as in a traditional class.

In British literature, eleven students and their teacher, a former English teacher at a public high school, were simultaneously working through *The Canterbury Tales* and *A Tale of Two Cities*. The class started with some pretty typical stuff: The students worked through a vocabulary lesson and defined "advent," "blasé," and "bravado," among other words. Students then split up into small groups to work on presentations on individual Tales to the class. They used a graphic organizer worksheet that prompted them to identify the main characters, summarize the plot, explain the moral of the story, and create five questions to ask their classmates. The groups worked through "The Nun's Priest Tale," "The Knight's Tale," and "The Wife of Bath's Tale" before the bell rang.

In a conversation as the students filed out, the teacher stated that she taught the class very similarly to how she had taught it in a traditional school, using the same materials but progressing at a faster pace. Because students have so much more time for reading at home, they could cover much more material than in a literature class at a five-day-a-week school. She noted that she could tell they had completed the reading by the way they discussed the books.

It was clear what might attract a teacher to the hybrid homeschooling model. Both classes were relaxed. Students hadn't been to school the day before and wouldn't be going to school the day after, so they seemed rested and not stressed about keeping up with the assignments. In both classes, teachers were able to teach at a high level and move quickly through the material, with most students keeping up and engaging with what was going on. There were no apparent discipline problems, and a sense of warmth at the school that made it a pleasant place to spend time. There is a lot to be said for that.

But just like hybrid homeschools aren't for every student or family, they aren't for every teacher. Few teachers, at least in private hybrid homeschools, can make do without outside financial support, either through a spouse's income or an additional job. This seems to be less of a challenge at public hybrid homeschools, where teachers' duties can expand to fill a full-time position at full-time pay, either by overseeing more hybrid students, also teaching in a school or district's full-time program, or building out their role into full-time hours in some other way.

If hybrid homeschooling is to grow, figuring out a compensation model that makes teaching more attractive to more traditional applicants seems like a good first step. But there are plenty of other policy issues to consider, which we'll examine in chapter 5.

NOTES

1. Andy Smarick, "Can Catholic Schools Be Saved?" *National Affairs* 45 (Spring 2011), https://www.nationalaffairs.com/publications/detail/can-catholic-schools-be-saved (accessed October 20, 2020).

2. National Catholic Education Association, "Catholic School Data." *NCEA.org*, 2020, https://www.ncea.org/ncea/proclaim/catholic_school_data/catholic_school_data.aspx (accessed October 20, 2020).

5

THE POWER OF POLICY

The Michigan Office of Financial Management's 2019–2020 Pupil Accounting Manual is a detailed, 171-page document. On its cover, there is a photo of a steam locomotive puffing grey-black smoke as it trundles through fall foliage toward the camera. In the foreground, we see the back of a deer crossing the tracks. It is staring at the oncoming train.

Behind this moody cover is the "Bible of Schools," according to Sharon Haynes, the program director of the Berrien Springs Parent Partnership, which enrolls homeschool students in local public-school classes according to this policy, from Section 5-E:

> A nonpublic pupil who attends a private, denominational, or parochial school, or a homeschooled pupil, may be enrolled on a part-time basis in nonessential elective courses provided by a public school district. This type of enrollment is referred to as shared-time enrollment because the pupil is enrolled in the public district and the nonpublic school or homeschool on a part-time basis.[1]

This flexibility, and the state funding that supports it, has allowed numerous Michigan districts to create hybrid homeschooling programs that formalize part-time enrollment in public schools as part of a student's education.

The Berrien Springs program provides elective classes to homeschool students in three counties in southern Michigan west of Kalamazoo: Berrien, Cass, and Van Buren. Students can take as many as four classes per semester for free, including as many as two credit-bearing college classes for older students. The state covers the costs.

Haynes, a former homeschool parent herself, recalled the program's origin story as a lesson in "why not?" thinking.

> It started with an interested homeschooling parent just thinking out of the box and going from district to district looking for the right fit and a willing administration. That's key in every single partnership that you would talk to. It usually takes a parent, a passionate parent. It takes a willing, open-minded district that is a good fit and is willing to take some risk, because at that time, the superintendent didn't see it as that risky, because he's like, "Well, there's nothing against it, so why can't we be for it? So nobody is saying we can't do this, and there's interpretation. There's lots of room for interpretation in the People Accounting Manual, so why not?"

Sitting at the intersection of interested parents and willing administrators is public policy. Laws and regulations will grease the gears or toss sand into them. When it comes to hybrid homeschooling, there are six areas of policy that contribute to either a nurturing or hostile environment:

1. homeschooling laws
2. private school regulations and accreditation requirements
3. competency-based education frameworks
4. part-time enrollment statutes
5. charter school authorizing and regulation
6. private school choice programs

Each of these can be used to create a permission structure for hybrid homeschooling to exist. And each can be used to prevent it from ever getting off the ground. It is worth examining all six.

HOMESCHOOLING LAWS

Why was Texas an early hotspot for hybrid homeschooling? Christy Wilson of Fort Worth's Alliance Christian Academy attributes it to the state's homeschooling laws. Said Wilson,

> The reality is that Texas has no laws necessarily regarding homeschooling, no regulations. So it is one of the easier states to be able to homeschool. The freedom to homeschool your students, or do a hybrid school, or do really anything

you choose is much easier in the state of Texas than it is in other places where you have to submit curriculum, you have to submit standardized test scores, all of those regulations.

The Homeschool Legal Defense Association (HSLDA) classifies state homeschooling regulations into four groups based on the requirements each imposes: "no notice required" and low, moderate, and high regulation.[2]

Texas is a "no notice required" state. To homeschool legally, Texas families do not have to inform their local school district or any other government official that they plan to teach children at home. Instead, they simply must teach four required subjects: math, reading, spelling and grammar, and good citizenship, using some form of written curriculum. This meets the definition of homeschooling in a "bona fide" manner and satisfies the legal precedents set by the Texas Supreme Court. Parents do not have to meet any specific teacher qualifications, students do not need to be assessed, and parents do not need to provide evidence of student immunizations. One in five U.S. states do not require homeschoolers to notify authorities of their plans; the others are Connecticut, Idaho, Illinois, Indiana, Iowa, Michigan, Missouri, New Jersey, and Oklahoma.

Wisconsin is considered a "low-regulation" state. To legally homeschool, families must file an annual report with the state Department of Public Instruction that lists how many children are enrolled in the homeschool and attests that the school will provide at least 875 hours of instruction and a "sequentially progressive" curriculum in reading, language arts, mathematics, social studies, science, and health, and affirms that the purpose of the school is home education and not simply to avoid compulsory attendance laws. Families are encouraged to keep records of their instructional hours and curriculum for their required subjects. About one in three U.S. states are considered low-regulation states; in addition to Wisconsin, they are Alabama, Arkansas, Arizona, California, Delaware, Georgia, Kansas, Kentucky, Mississippi, Montana, Nebraska, Nevada, New Mexico, Utah, and Wyoming. In some of these states, for example, California and Kansas, homeschools can act as a form of nonaccredited private school or home-based satellites of an existing private school that provides the curriculum and manages the record keeping.

Florida is an example of a "moderate-regulation" state. According to the state's homeschooling statute, families must send their local school district superintendent a notice of intent to homeschool that includes each student's name, birthdate, and home address. Families must maintain a portfolio of educational records and work, including a log of the student's activities and samples of student projects. The local school superintendent can request to review this portfolio, and parents must keep it for at least two years after it was completed. Students also must participate in annual education evaluations to assess their academic progress. Families can meet this requirement by having students take a state or national test under the supervision of a certified teacher or having a certified teacher of their choosing review a portfolio of work and interview the student. About one in three U.S. states have moderate homeschooling regulations, including Colorado, Louisiana, Maine, Maryland, Minnesota, New Hampshire, North Carolina, North Dakota, Ohio, Oregon, South Carolina, South Dakota, Tennessee, Virginia, Washington, and West Virginia, in addition to Florida.

Massachusetts is considered a "high-regulation" state. Massachusetts homeschooling families need to file an annual notice of intent to homeschool and detail the proposed curriculum, number of hours of instruction, textbooks and instructional materials, methods of assessment, and parents' competency to serve as educators. Families must demonstrate that they are teaching students spelling; reading; writing; English language and grammar; geography; arithmetic; drawing; music; U.S. history and the Constitution; and the duties of citizenship, health, physical education, and "good behavior." Local districts can require students to participate in standardized testing, but families often can submit progress reports and portfolios of student work to meet requirements. Just five U.S. states are in this high-regulation category, including New York, Pennsylvania, Rhode Island, Massachusetts, and Vermont.

These laws can either foster or smother burgeoning hybrid homeschools. In many cases, the first iteration of a hybrid homeschool is a more informal co-op, while the necessary legal work is done to create and register the organization as a private school. In high-regulation states, heavy restrictions on what is taught and for how long can prevent the kinds of innovation that hybrid homeschools look to foster. Detailed rules and reporting requirements also can create a barrier to entry for parents, who may opt simply to send their children to an established private school or keep their kids in public school rather than risk running afoul of a lengthy and byzantine law.

PRIVATE SCHOOL REGULATIONS AND ACCREDITATION

Many hybrid homeschooling leaders will emphasize that they are not operating a "school." True, this is partially to give a nod to parents, who leaders recognize as the primary educators of the children in their care. They want to be clear that they are supplementing what parents are doing, not replacing it. But there is a more picayune reason as well: regulations.

Here's how Keri Beckman, executive director of the Regina Caeli Academy, explained the way this issue plays out in her hybrid homeschool network. Regina Caeli serves eleven hundred students in eleven states, all of whom attend class on campus two days a week. But, she cautioned, it's not a "school." She further stated,

> They do wear uniforms, and it may look like a school. But it is not a school, and the reason—well, a couple of reasons. One, we don't meet the legal qualifications, if you will, or the criteria of, you need 185 days. We meet twice a week for thirty-two weeks. And then the other part of it is, we want the parents to remain the primary educators because we believe strongly that the family is the best formation for the person. And so, if we were to take on more of those hours in the academy setting, the peers then would start to be forming each other, rather than the family forming, being the peer influence there.

This is more than a philosophical debate: Private schools are more highly regulated than most people realize, and programs like Beckman's want to preserve the family-led flexibility that inspired them in the first place. Almost every state regulates the length of the school year. States like Idaho, Maine, and Pennsylvania require private-school teachers to be certified. Some states require that the private schools provide instruction in English and that the curricula they use be similar to that of public schools, including covering the particular state's history or constitution and teaching such specific subjects as reading, writing, math, science, and social studies. These rules are on top of general regulations regarding student health and safety, vaccination requirements, and equal access for minority students.

This can get into controversial territory. For example, the Illinois Critical Health Problems and Comprehensive Health Education Act requires that schools, both public and private, teach a health course that includes "studies in human growth and development, family life instruction, AIDS education (grades 6–12), alcohol, tobacco, and drug abuse."[3] There is an opt-out provision for parents but not schools. South Dakota's private schooling laws require that,

> Moral and character instruction must be given in all nonpublic elementary and secondary schools that is intended to impress upon the minds of students the importance of citizenship, patriotism, honesty, self-discipline, self-respect, sexual abstinence, respect for the contributions of minority and ethnic groups

to the heritage of South Dakota, regard for the elderly, and respect for authority.[4]

Some states require the accreditation of private schools. Others simply require schools to register. Others require some form of licensing, and still others require state approval for new private schools. Private schools also must hew to state vaccination laws for school-age children, which can run afoul of some families' preferences.

These can shape whether hybrid homeschools can or would want to open in those states. If the curriculum requirement is too prescriptive, schools that teach via such integrated subjects as logic and rhetoric, as in the case of classical schools, or via the practical arts in more progressive Waldorf-model schools could find themselves running into problems. Exacting requirements about seat time or instructional hours can get crossways of hybrid homeschools as well.

Many hybrid homeschools have worked with accrediting agencies for an outside seal of approval, for instance, UMSI, or University Model Schools International. "I knew that if we were going to rise above the reputation and the belief that the university model is a homeschool co-op, we would have to be accredited," Barbara Freedman, USMI's CEO, said. She has worked for years with various bodies to gain accreditation; the Southern Association of Colleges and Schools accredited Grace Prep in the fall of 2003, and the corporation was accredited through the organization that became known as AdvancED in 2006. Freedman is working toward a systems accreditation, which will allow USMI to work with AdvancED to accredit all eighty of its schools. All of this has been done to, in Freeman's words, give the USMI brand more credibility and maintain the identity and integrity of their school model.

COMPETENCY-BASED EDUCATION

Flemingsburg, Kentucky, sits about an hour east of Lexington. To get there, you drive along a few small state roads surrounded mostly by open land. Eventually, you'll pass by a large tan brick building on the outskirts of the small downtown—Fleming County High School.

This may not be the first place you'd imagine an innovative hybrid homeschool would take off. But it is home to the Fleming County Performance Academy, a homeschool options program that allows local families to attend a full-time virtual course of study or participate in a hybrid model where children attend classes in person for some portion of the school week.

How are they able to do this? Fleming County takes advantage of Kentucky's competency-based standards, according to which students can earn credits by demonstrating mastery of a subject, rather than participating in a set number of instructional hours. Fleming County Schools superintendent Brian Creasman, who was named Kentucky's superintendent of the year in 2020, describes the options available to them as such:

> We have performance-based or instructional seat time. So, if we enroll them in the performance mastery program here in Kentucky, they do not have to have instructional seat time, those Carnegie units. So it was sort of like it's been staring us in the face, and we just decided to opt to use it.

Schools have been traditionally governed by the Carnegie Unit, named for the 120-hour standard that the Carnegie Foundation required university professors to meet to qualify for the pensions it funded. Prior to that effort, mastery of subject matter was determined by ad hoc assessments created by teachers and professors. These assessments became victims of the standardization revolution that defined the Progressive Age at the turn of the twentieth century.

It didn't stop at universities. After setting the seat time standard in 1906, the foundation was able to influence nearly every high school in the United States to adopt the same definition. To hit 120 hours, a class would need to meet 5 days a week for 45 minutes for 32 weeks of the year. Some schools used longer, less frequent classes, and some went shorter and more frequent, but the 120-hour total remained constant.

Throughout time, educators chafed against the strictures of the Carnegie Unit and called for students who were able to demonstrate that they had mastered material to be able to move on without meeting a specified number of instructional minutes or hours. States responded by granting flexibility for schools to assess student knowledge and use that as the basis for advancement. Sometimes states grant waivers to seat-time requirements for schools or districts that want to use a competency-based assessment process. Others, like Kentucky, offer different pathways for demonstrating student progress and allow schools and districts to choose between them. More than thirty U.S. states allow competency-based learning; however, according to the education nonprofit Achieve, "Policies do not always translate into broad use by districts and schools, where traditional definitions of credit as seat time prevail in local policy and practice."[5]

The flexibility and opportunity to personalize student learning in a competency-based framework is a necessary precondition for public hybrid homeschools. Hybrid homeschools do not meet seat-time requirements, so they must be able to demonstrate that their students are meeting necessary benchmarks some other way.

PART-TIME ENROLLMENT STATUTES

Interstate 25 runs parallel to the Front Range of the Rocky Mountains, a north-to-south slice through the center of Colorado. It connects the greater Denver conurbation that stretches from Fort Collins to Colorado Springs. An archipelago of public hybrid homeschools has popped up along the route and spread from there into the snowcapped mountains that rise to the West.

Why Colorado? One of the strongest reasons is the state's part-time enrollment law. Schools can opt to enroll homeschool students on a part-time basis and receive about half of the per-pupil state aid amount for each of those students. The rules are relatively flexible, allowing districts to include students in part-time headcounts so long as they participate in 90 to 360 hours of teacher contact during the course of a 1,080-hour school year. (For context, the state's homeschool law requires 688 hours of instruction per year.) Students who spend more than 360 hours in pupil–teacher instruction are considered full-time pupils, and districts get the full per-pupil state aid amount for them. Those who participate in fewer than 90 hours of instruction do not count in terms of funding.

This creates a strong incentive for schools to create hybrid programs where children attend classes in person for some amount of time, particularly at the lower end of the range that qualifies for funding. That way, schools can bank the difference between what they spend and what they receive. One Colorado charter school leader, who shared this detail on the condition they not be identified, explained the math: By providing just one day of instruction per week, a school can receive state aid for a part-time enrolled student who paid for two-and-a-half days' worth of instruction. Hybrid homeschooling helps bring in revenue that supports overall school programs. They went on to say the following:

> On the business side at the charter school, funding's really tight. We took a look at the one day's worth of education for two and a half days' worth of funding, and it was just a really good business decision to say, if we bring

this program in, we can take 80 percent of the money. Eighty percent of the money that we get from the state will go back into the homeschool program, 20 percent of it will go back to the school as general revenue.

Michigan takes a slightly different approach. Students are allowed to take "nonessential" courses, that is, courses outside of the "core" courses of math, science, social studies, and English-language arts. Rather than using Colorado's zero, half-, or full-time funding mechanism, the Pupil Accounting Manual instructs schools to calculate a student's full-time equivalence, or whatever fraction of a typical day that they spend in school. So, if, for example, a district's year includes 180 days of six periods, each lasting 55 minutes long, that works out to 350 minutes of instruction per day, or 1,050 instructional hours for the year. If a homeschool student enrolls in a class that meets for 55 minutes three days per week, that totals 99 hours of instruction and qualifies for state reimbursement of about 9 percent of per-pupil funding for full-time students.

The shape of part-time enrollment statutes will govern the kinds of public hybrid homeschool models that emerge. If a state regulates what classes students can and cannot take, it will determine what classes are available to homeschoolers. How the state generates the fraction of funding that a part-time student generates will determine how substantial hybrid programs can be. All of these decisions have tradeoffs, and there are turf wars to be fought.

CHARTER AUTHORIZING AND REGULATIONS

During a 1988 speech at the National Press Club in Washington, D.C., Albert Shanker, the influential American Federation of Teachers president, claimed that "80 percent of students do not learn well in traditional settings."[6] He encouraged the "bottom-up" reform efforts throughout the country that were "trying to build something new . . . that will be effective for more than the 10 or 15 or 20 percent of the students who have been able to learn throughout history." Building on the work of Ray Budde of the University of Massachusetts at Amherst, among others, Shanker put his weight behind the idea of a charter school. According to Shanker,

> Do not think of a school as a building, and you can see how it works. Consider 6 or 7 or 12 teachers in a school who say, "We've got an idea. We've got a way of doing something very different. We've got a way of reaching the kids that are now not being reached by what the school is doing."

Enterprising educators and legislators in Minnesota built on this vision, passing the first charter-school law in 1991, and opening the first charter schools in 1992. That movement has now grown to more than 6,000 schools and 3 million students throughout the county.

Hybrid homeschools would appear to meet many of the characteristics that Shanker laid out more than thirty years ago. They are designed to reach students who do not learn well in traditional schooling environments. While many are private, others work within the public-school system. And almost all were founded by a small group of passionate educators and families looking for a "way of doing something very different."

The charter-school sector writ large has not generated the diversity of offerings that initial backers might have hoped for. In a 2015 paper, Jenn Hatfield and I examined the composition of charter schools in seventeen different American cities and classified them based on their offerings.[7] We found that a little more than half of charter schools had no distinguishing characteristics and no particular pedagogical focus. Of "specialized" charter schools, the largest category was so-called "no excuses" schools, followed by "progressive" schools and then credit-recovery high schools. This is not exactly the radical rethinking that early proponents of the charter model had in mind.

What accounts for this relative lack of educational diversity? One is the charter authorizing process itself. The "charter" in charter schools refers to the agreement that school leaders draft with whatever authorizing body is tasked with holding charters accountable for the promises that they make. The source of this oversight varies from state to state, ranging from state department of education bureaucrats to local school district leaders. One near-constant, however, is the mountain of paperwork that prospective charter school operators have to complete to gain authorization, which I researched for another 2015 paper written with Jenn Hatfield and Elizabeth English.[8] Many states require multihundred-page applications, which serve as a barrier to entry. Authorizers also regularly reject applications for schools for a variety of reasons, including that they don't think the proposed school is the right fit. Prejudices from charter authorizers about what makes a "good" school can prevent new and different models from emerging.

For there to be more charter hybrid homeschools, authorizers need to be more flexible. They need to realize that their sector is supposed to foster innovation and encourage educators to try new and different things. Charter schools emerged as a new way to reach the 80 percent of children who are not learning as well as they can in their typical school environment.

There has been a great deal of path dependence in charter-school authorizing, with swift approvals of familiar models and an easier path for established providers. Innovators have been viewed skeptically. Given that authorizers are granting the use of millions of public dollars and allowing hundreds of children to attend a school, their hesitancy is understandable. At the same time, path dependency can breed groupthink, and promising nontraditional models can be denied the fair shake they deserve.

But the problem is not just with authorizers. Many states are changing charter-school regulations in ways that will affect hybrid models.

Perhaps no state has put charters more in the crosshairs than California, and recent efforts to change laws there have threatened the operational autonomy that charter schools have. In 2019, Governor Gavin Newsom signed two such bills into law: AB 1505 and AB 1507. AB 1505 dramatically expanded the power of local school districts to approve or deny charter applications. Most critically, a district now can reject a charter school application if it can prove that opening the charter will have a negative fiscal effect on district finances. Almost every district, and particularly those in tough financial straits, will be able to demonstrate this and stop the growth and expansion of charter schools in their area.

The law also increased restrictions on charters: It introduced new credentialing requirements for teachers, who previously had much more flexibility to teach without state certification, and added stricter rules about student performance related to charter renewal. If a school has been classified in one of the two lowest performance categories or scored below the statewide averages on annual tests, it will not be renewed.

The other law, AB 1507, specifically targeted nontraditional charter schools, including hybrid programs. Previously, hybrid schools were able to operate learning centers in counties adjacent to their authorizing district. For example, outside San Diego, the Julian Charter Schools network offers various hybrid options for homeschoolers, including monthly support for parent-led learning, a virtual charter school, supervised independent study, and brick-and-mortar academies that homeschool students attend two days a week. These activities occur at a variety of locations in several different jurisdictions, which ruffled the feathers of the leaders of school districts in these counties.

That flexibility is going away. Now school districts will have to approve any buildings within their district boundaries. As the California Charter Schools Association put it, "Many schools may have to consider restructuring or reauthorizing to comply with this bill."[9]

What does this mean for hybrid schools? According to multiple hybrid charter-school leaders, the financial impact stipulation will be a next-to-impossible hurdle to overcome—any district that doesn't want a charter school can easily reject applications. It is not hard for a district to show a negative financial impact, so it will be a catchall for charter-skeptical school boards.

In addition, the teacher credentialing rules threaten hybrid schools because they often have teachers work across subjects and grade levels based on student needs. That will be more difficult to do now. Leaders also say the updated definitions of necessary student progress will be a challenge for credit-recovery programs or any hybrid that serves at-risk kids. What happens if they take credit-deficient students or students who are many years behind their peers? If those students cannot get their total school scores above average (which by definition half of schools will not be able to), the school is at risk of getting closed down.

PRIVATE SCHOOL CHOICE PROGRAMS

Twenty-nine states, the District of Columbia, and Puerto Rico operate private school choice programs, which provide public funding for families who send their children to private school.[10] These programs take three major forms. First is the best known: school vouchers. Voucher programs give parents part of the public funding that would have paid for their child to attend public school in the form of a coupon, which families can use to pay for their child's private-school tuition.

Less well known, but more numerous, are tax credit scholarship programs. Per these programs, individuals or corporations can donate to nonprofit organizations that grant private-school scholarships to students. The donors are then partially or fully reimbursed in the form of a tax credit. Families seeking scholarships apply to the organization, not the state, and the dollars that fund scholarships never touch the public purse. In addition, some states also offer credits or deductions for families who are paying private-school tuition that decrease their tax liability or tax bill.

About a half-dozen states offer a new sort of private school choice program, education savings accounts. This is separate from well-known 529 or Coverdell savings accounts; rather, these programs return some of the public funds that would have been spent on a student's education to his or her family. States deposit the funds into a flexible-use spending account that operates much like a health savings account to cover applicable expenses

THE POWER OF POLICY

for homeschooling, private-school and college tuition, tutoring, and curricula and materials. Families are restricted in where they can spend their dollars, and vendors must be approved by the state.

Historically, homeschool advocacy groups have had a chilly relationship with the school choice movement. The HSLDA writes on its website that it "opposes any government money to homeschool families, whether these handouts are called vouchers, education savings accounts, or any other term." It continues, "HSLDA believes that such money would be a handout from the government, which will eventually lead to regulations that will restrict homeschool freedom."[11]

Many hybrid homeschoolers look at private-school program with hesitancy. Consider Christ Prep in Lenexa, Kansas, where students attend class on campus three days a week and work at home the other two. Kansas has a growing tax credit scholarship program that awarded almost 1,000 scholarships worth $3.6 million through the 2018–2019 school year. But Christ Prep is not part of the five-year-old program—at least not yet. Principal Ron Lawlor worries that "if you participate in some things, you open the door wide to a whole set of requirements, some of which can, on occasion, become troublesome." He expanded to say,

> We have not really participated in the kinds of things that would require us to do things that we feel like we're just not equipped to do. Again, not that we don't want to do them, we just feel like at this point in the journey we were not equipped, we're not prepared to do that. Christ Prep, for example, is not in a place to administer individual education plans for every student.

But Lawlor did describe the tax credit scholarship program as more "light touch" and spoke of a willingness to potentially participate in the future.

THE MAP AND THE TERRITORY

If you want to know about school choice policy and hybrid homeschooling, you'd be hard-pressed to find a better resource than Wes Cantrell. Cantrell is a member of the Georgia House of Representatives and cofounder of a hybrid homeschool on the outskirts of suburban Atlanta, the King's Academy. The school enrolls almost one thousand students, who combine homeschooling with on-campus classes two or three days a week, including a small number from low-income families who use Georgia's tax credit scholarship program to attend.

When asked if he thought the school would participate in something like an education savings account program, he responded with a resounding yes. Because tuition at the King's Academy is relatively low, ranging from $3,900 to $4,600 based on grade level, a state-run savings account program would essentially cover the entire cost.

Cantrell explained,

> It would be great for a school like ours, because if the family could just get the state money . . . that would basically cover a year's worth of tuition. . . . I think the average private school is like $12,000 or $14,000 to $16,000 a year in Georgia. So you're just getting them halfway there in the other cases. But in our case, it would pay almost the entire amount.

School choice policies have the power to help or hinder hybrid homeschools. Should hybrid homeschoolers seem themselves as part of the school choice movement? If so, should they join the coalition of private schools that advocate for increased support for their students?

The answer to the first question is an obvious yes. Families choose hybrid homeschools. They are schools of choice. Thus, they should see themselves as part of a broader movement. As to the second, it's a tougher sell. But hybrid homeschoolers should advocate for themselves alongside private schools as well.

Too many hybrid homeschoolers have a mistaken belief that if they stay out of the contentious politics of school choice they are going to be left alone. But numerous highly placed researchers and authors believe that homeschooling should be presumptively banned and are willing to make those arguments in widely read publications. No less than the nation's largest labor union, the National Education Association states as its current policy that, "Homeschooling programs based on parental choice cannot provide the student with a comprehensive education experience." It fought for years to make homeschooling illegal and now advocates for a raft of regulations that would eliminate most of the things that make homeschools unique from public schools. These include requiring the "taking and passing of assessments to ensure adequate academic progress" and "instruction . . . by persons who are licensed by the appropriate state education licensure agency," as well as a "curriculum approved by the state department of education."[12]

In addition, private schooling continues to find its way into the crosshairs. The influential political website FiveThirtyEight ran a column in May 2019, entitled "Political Confessional: I Think Private Schools Should Be

Banned."[13] In an interview with the *Atlantic* published with the title "Are Private Schools Immoral?" MacArthur "Genius Grant" fellow and Pulitzer Prize–winning journalist Nikole Hannah-Jones was asked whether she would ban private schools if she was made dictator of the United States. "The answer to your question is yes, you would have to," she responded. "If you truly wanted to equalize and integrate schools, you would have to."[14] In 2019, the British Labour Party went so far as including the banning of private schools and the confiscation of their assets as a plank of its policy manifesto.[15]

Hybrid homeschools have a foot in both homeschooling and private schooling. As their profile grows, they should not be surprised to see the ire turned on them. This makes building coalitions with both groups especially important to securing their futures. The larger the coalition, the more likely they will be able to repel legal and political incursions. If they choose to stand alone, they are in that much more vulnerable of a position.

In addition, legislators can craft private school choice policies to protect the autonomy of hybrid homeschools while providing the support that their students need. Ron Lawlor pointed to one method, tax credit scholarships. Rather than vouchers, which require the state to directly fund scholarships for students, tax credit scholarship programs leave the management to nonprofit scholarship-granting organizations. Donors give their own private dollars to these private organizations, which then award private scholarships to individual students attending private schools. True, some states place restrictions on who can get scholarships and create some hoops that schools have to jump through to receive scholarship students, but the burden is far less than in voucher programs.

Those sorts of rules matter. In a survey of 954 school leaders in three states, researchers Brian Kisida, Patrick Wolf, and Evan Rhinesmith found widely diverging rates of participation in private school choice programs. In Florida, which has a tax credit scholarship program, 60 percent of private schools participated. But in Indiana and Louisiana, which have voucher programs, the rates were much lower: only half of private schools in Indiana and only a third of private schools in Louisiana.[16] The number-one concern of participating school leaders in both Indiana and Louisiana was "future regulations that might come with participation"—which was also the number-one reason cited by school leaders in all three states who had declined to participate in any taxpayer-supported choice program. By contrast, the top concern for participating Florida school leaders was that the "scholarship program will end." A stark difference.

Education savings accounts, what Wes Cantrell thought would benefit the King's Academy, are another tool to provide support without overly entangling the government. In those programs, state education agencies or treasurer's offices create a list of approved vendors where families can spend their dollars. Because not all of the vendors are traditional schools (some are physical therapy providers, tutoring services, or a host of other educators), the types of requirements that states impose are more flexible. Vendors have to demonstrate that they actually provide the services that they advertise, but families have more latitude to include unique and different experiences in their children's education. Either of these types of programs could expand the set of students that hybrid homeschools serve without curtailing schools' unique missions and methods.

NOTES

1. Michigan Office of Financial Management, "Pupil Accounting Manual 2019–20," 5-E-1. *Michigan.gov*, 2020, https://www.michigan.gov/documents/mde/2019-20_Pupil_Accounting_Manual_672533_7.pdf (accessed October 20, 2020).
2. Homeschool Legal Defense Association, "Homeschool Laws by State." *HSLDA.org*, 2020, https://hslda.org/legal (accessed October 20, 2020).
3. U.S. Department of Education, "State Regulation of Private Schools," 76. *Ed.gov*, 2009, https://www2.ed.gov/admins/comm/choice/regprivschl/regprivschl.pdf (accessed October 20, 2020).
4. U.S. Department of Education, "State Regulation of Private Schools," 254.
5. Susan Patrick and Chris Sturgis, "Cracking the Code: Synchronizing Policy and Practice to Support Personalized Learning." *iNACOL*, July 2011, https://files.eric.ed.gov/fulltext/ED537322.pdf (accessed October 20, 2020).
6. Albert Shanker, "National Press Club Speech: Albert Shanker, President, American Federation of Teachers Washington, D.C." *Reuther.wayne.edu*, March 31, 1988, https://reuther.wayne.edu/files/64.43.pdf (accessed October 20, 2020).
7. Michael Q. McShane and Jenn Hatfield, "Measuring Diversity in Charter School Offerings." *American Enterprise Institute*, March 1, 1988, https://www.aei.org/research-products/report/measuring-diversity-in-charter-school-offerings/ (accessed October 20, 2020).
8. Michael Q. McShane, Jenn Hatfield, and Elizabeth English. "The Paperwork Pile-Up: Measuring the Burden of Charter School Applications." *American Enterprise Institute*, May 19, 2015, https://www.aei.org/research-products/report/the-paperwork-pile-up-measuring-the-burden-of-charter-school-applications/?utm_source=paramount&utm_medium=email&utm_campaign=mediamcshanecharterschoolapplications&utm_content=report (accessed October 20, 2020).

9. California Charter Schools Association, "A Summary of AB 1505 and AB 1507." *Hubspot.net*, https://cdn2.hubspot.net/hubfs/3049635/AB%201505_1507%20Brief.pdf?__hssc=206422988.1.1590069663186&__hstc=206422988.b4d7fc4011ed8f1b0ccb23dd7f559dfa.1590069663185.1590069663185.1590069663185.1&__hsfp=946197843&hsCtaTracking=7b7ef75f-12f1-485d-a697-34ff26e21f67%7C8b85d1ef-73ba-4e81-9dbd-aca65d956fc8 (accessed October 20, 2020).

10. EdChoice, "The ABCs of School Choice: 2020 Edition." *EdChoice.org*, January 22, 2020, https://www.edchoice.org/research/the-abcs-of-school-choice/ (accessed October 20, 2020).

11. Homeschool Legal Defense Association, "Vouchers." *NCHE.HSLDA.org*, 2020, http://nche.hslda.org/docs/nche/Issues/S/State_Vouchers.asp (accessed October 20, 2020).

12. National Education Association (2020) *2020-21 Resolutions*. pg. 37 Accessed December 2, 2020 at https://www.nea.org/about-nea/governance-policies/nea-resolutions .

13. Clare Malone, "Political Confession: I Think Private Schools Should Be Banned." *Fivethirtyeight*, April 29, 2019, https://fivethirtyeight.com/features/political-confessional-i-think-private-schools-should-be-banned/ (accessed October 21, 2020).

14. Dianna Douglas, "Are Private Schools Immoral?" *Atlantic*, December 14, 2017, https://www.theatlantic.com/education/archive/2017/12/progressives-are-undermining-public-schools/548084/ (accessed October 21, 2020).

15. Benjamin Kentish, "Labour Votes to Abolish Private Schools at Party Conference." *Independent*, September 22, 2019, https://www.independent.co.uk/news/uk/politics/labour-public-private-school-abolish-eton-vote-conference-corbyn-education-policy-a9115766.html (accessed October 21, 2020).

16. Brian Kisida, Patrick Wolf, and Evan Rhinesmith, "Views from Private Schools: Attitudes about School Choice Programs in Three States." *American Enterprise Institute*, January 2015, https://www.aei.org/wp-content/uploads/2015/01/Views-from-Private-Schools-7.pdf (accessed October 21, 2020).

6

THE PROCESS OF INNOVATION

Père Lachaise, in Paris's 20th arrondissement, is the most visited cemetery on earth. Ambling through its curved cobblestone paths of limestone ossuaries is akin to wandering through the histories of literature, art, and science. Medieval lovers Abelard and Heloise are there. Composers Frederic Chopin and Georges Bizet are, too. The Irish poet, playwright, critic, and bon vivant Oscar Wilde's plinth is pockmarked with kisses of red lipstick.

A less-visited and more moss-covered vault belongs to Jean-Baptist Say, an economist born in Lyon in 1767. Say gifted the French language, and in turn the English language, with the term *entrepreneur*. He wrote, "The entrepreneur shifts economic resources out of an area of lower and into an area of higher productivity and greater yield."[1] Since Say was laid in his final resting place in 1832, near the end of the Industrial Revolution, millions of entrepreneurs have used technology and human ingenuity to remake the world in ways he could have never imagined.

Hybrid homeschoolers have done that for their children's educations. They are educational entrepreneurs. They take resources that traditional systems have been using poorly, for instance, funding, manpower, and buildings, and shift their use to serve students better. Because these are schools of choice, the proof is in their popularity. Parents don't have to enroll their children in hybrid homeschools. Yet, they continue to do so, and as homeschooling grows in popularity, demand for these arrangements appears to be growing as well.

Hybrid homeschooling can teach us about entrepreneurship in education and the engine that drives it: innovation. That is the topic of this final substantive chapter, which explores the development and diffusion of hybrid homeschooling through the lens of design thinking and adoption patterns. In exploring these frames, two major lessons will emerge. First, *start with people and their problems*. And second, *focus on solving a small number of big problems*. With these approaches, innovators can offer a disruptive educational approach that more families will be ready to embrace.

We stand on the shoulders of giants, so it should be noted here that this endeavor builds on the work of homeschooling scholars like Mitchell Stevens, who presciently writes in *Kingdom of Children*,

> Entrepreneurs do not work in vacuums. Just as in business, where particular regulatory environments, fluctuating market conditions, and spotty information require opportunity-takers to be knowledgeable and nimble, in the business of social movements entrepreneurs must do their work in a manner that is sensitive to context. The factors that shape the fate of movement-builders are numerous. Some are structural: the legal organization of a society, for example, which determines the outside costs of doing things unconventionally and provides the rules for voicing official dissent. Some are cultural: the intellectual traditions that shape the heads of potential recruits; the larger culture's stock of legitimate ways of making sense of things; and the organizational sensibilities that characterize people's sense of how they can appropriately be glued together into groups.[2]

DESIGN THINKING

Design thinking has revolutionized the development of the products that we use every day. Pioneered by Nobel Laureate Herbert A. Simon in the 1970s, design thinking focuses first on a user's experience with a product. This human-centered approach starts with a thorough understanding of how people will interact with and use a product and then creates and refines that product by questioning, testing, and adjusting in a constant process of improvement. Rikke Friis Dam and Teo Yu Siang of the Interaction Design Foundation describe it as a "process in which we seek to understand the user, challenge assumptions, and redefine problems in an attempt to identify alternative strategies and solutions that might not be instantly apparent with our initial level of understanding."[3]

Whether they intend to be or not, hybrid homeschoolers are a great example of design thinking. Take Hallmark Charter School in Sanger,

California—a hybrid charter that began as a last-chance program for the "kids the system didn't want," according to Principal Alfred Sanchez. Originally, students who had been expelled or suspended, or had dropped out of traditional schools, were told to work through an independent study course and check in with a teacher for one hour each week. Not surprisingly, many students were not thriving in this hands-off environment. So, Hallmark looked closely at its students' experiences and needs, and began creating the classes and programs that would connect them to their school.

Many students were budding graffiti artists, so Hallmark took over a nearby art gallery and taught in-person classes there. It added math and science tutorials, built a partnership with a local public high school so students could play sports, and added a live music program. "We became an art factory," Sanchez said, with students winning art contests and showcasing their work for the community.

Eventually Hallmark formalized these offerings and became a true hybrid homeschool program. Students have to come to campus two days per week and take at least two math classes in person, each lasting one hour. They have flexibility as to the days and times they take their classes, but formal, regular contact is required, and it keeps them on pace with their studies.

Choices Charter School in Sacramento has a similar origin story. As principal Tony Oddo says, "I can take kids who have made mistakes." In 1998, Choices started out as an alternative program with an independent study model for students who had been expelled or pushed out of traditional schools. But students struggled, and the school leadership team explored ways to better support them.

In the ensuing years, Choices moved, as Oddo put it, "from credit recovery to AP." It started with one hour of live, in-person instruction per class per week and built from there, adding electives that students were interested in and eventually building a major visual and performing arts program. It now offers AP classes to serve the higher-performing students who have been attracted to Choices by the flexibility of its model.

In both of these cases, school leaders started with a deep appreciation of the needs and desires of their "users"—their students and their families. They continuously asked tough questions about their own offerings and what they could be doing better. They were flexible, and when a need arose for a particular kind of course or support structure, they created it.

In a 2018 article in *Harvard Business Review* titled "Why Design Thinking Works," Jeanne Liedtka, a professor at the University of Virginia's Darden School of Business, describes both the goals and methods of design thinking.[4] "To be successful," she argues, "an innovation process must deliver three things: superior solutions, lower risks and costs of change, and employee buy-in."

Hybrid homeschooling clears all three of these bars. Parents believe these schools are a superior solution. A simple examination of tuition levels shows that the cost of change is lower, as families have to risk far less money to try out a hybrid homeschool for a semester or a year. And, as we heard in chapter 4, educators by and large enjoy this model and buy into its purpose.

Liedtka describes seven actions organizations must take to maximize the impact of design thinking: immersion, sense-making, alignment, emergence, articulation, preexperience, and learning in action.

> *Immersion* involves deeply enmeshing product designers in the lives of their customers. Rather than making assumptions about who their customers are and what they want, great design thinkers try to walk a mile in their customers' shoes and understand their motivations, the problems they have, and, perhaps most importantly, the strengths and assets they bring to the table.
>
> *Sense-making* takes the insights from that immersion experience and spots patterns, themes, and commonalities.
>
> *Emergence* starts to brainstorm product ideas.
>
> During *articulation*, innovators pressure-test their ideas, questioning their own biases and assumptions.
>
> During *preexperience*, Liedtka recommends creating very basic, low-cost models of potential products that users can interact with to identify strengths and weaknesses.
>
> The seventh and final step is *learning in action*, or the constant process of evaluation and revision that innovators and their employees use to improve their products.

Hybrid homeschools have accomplished most of these steps informally. The designers of hybrid homeschools are typically homeschoolers themselves—their clients' lives and their lives are often one and the same. As they work together, they make sense of individual issues and find common themes, for example, the need for higher-level math and science instruction and activities. They then align around these common sets of problems and design courses and other school offerings to solve them, brainstorming and crafting novel solutions in living rooms and church basements. Finally, they launch hybrid schools, often just as a single grade, narrow grade band, or small number of classrooms, with the plan to learn as they grow.

These grassroots, student-centered innovations are responsive and show how hybrid programs can effectively meet their students' needs. But hybrid homeschoolers also could benefit from formalizing these processes. Especially in the articulation phase, when they are exploring the potential benefits and pitfalls of a proposed new model or program, many schools could benefit from more outside input. Oftentimes, schools are founded by a core group of families and educators based on their shared values and ideals, which may breed insularity. Opening their ideas to a broader community, where disagreement may be more likely, could help identify weak points or areas that could use further exploration.

The U.S. education system writ large could benefit from more design thinking. Here, hybrid homeschoolers and the educators that partner with them offer several lessons. Looking at the public school districts that have partnered with homeschoolers, it took school leaders that saw homeschooling parents as allies and not enemies. Rather than looking at them as weirdos who are outside of the mainstream of society, they recognized that these parents had legitimate criticisms of the traditional schooling system and tried to address those concerns.

What if that attitude was pervasive throughout education? What if educational administrators and policymakers more deeply enmeshed themselves in the communities that they serve and viewed their schools through the eyes of their parents and students? Schools would look different.

DIFFUSING INNOVATIONS

How do ideas spread? In 1962, Everett Rogers first published *Diffusion of Innovations*, an exhaustive study of how new ideas spread along communication networks and cycles of adoption. Featuring case studies of diverse innovations from kindergarten to water sanitation in a remote Peruvian village, Rogers highlights and explains the process of innovation for products and processes, and the way that those innovations take hold.[5]

To help explain how ideas spread, Rogers separates people into five categories based on when they adopt a new idea. Figure 6.1 shows how Rogers displays the categories and their relative size in the marketplace. As time progresses from left to right along the X-axis, more and more people adopt the idea.

Those first to a new idea, product, or service are the 2.5 percent of people called "innovators." As Rogers describes them, "The salient value of the innovator is venturesomeness, due to a desire for the rash, the daring, and the risky."[6] Innovators are the people who had Google Glass eyewear in 2014. They are the first to try something new, often before it hits the mass market, even though they understand that new products and services are rife with bugs and problems. They are comfortable working through the hiccups because they want to be on the bleeding edge. Innovators are the smallest contingent, as most people are not willing to put up with potential problems for novelty's sake.

The next category is "early adopters," who "decrease uncertainty about a new idea by adopting it and then convey a subjective evaluation of the innovation to near peers through interpersonal networks."[7] Most of us know someone like this. They are the first person in line to get the new iPhone or try a new app or service. They were the first to get a Facebook page or an Uber account. They try new innovations out and, if they like them, recommend them to friends and family, and the bulk of people who make up the next two categories of adopters.

The meat of the bell curve is made up of the two groups that emerge next on the timeline: "early majority" and "late majority" adopters. Those in the early majority "deliberate for some time before completely adopting a new idea" and want to kick the tires of a new product or new idea before purchasing it.[8] They collect opinions from early adopters and only choose once they are satisfied the innovation is ready for prime time. Those in the late majority share many of the same characteristics but are simply more risk averse. They "do not adopt until most others in their system have already done so."[9] Often they are forced to adopt an innovation due to its ubiquity

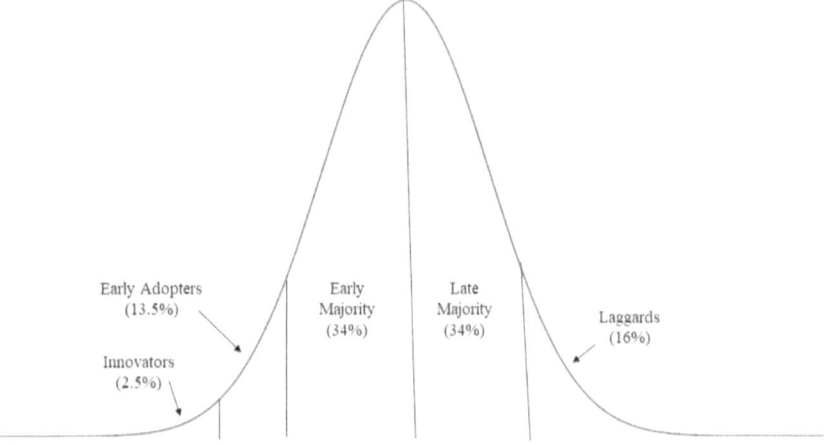

Figure 6.1. Rogers's Adoption Categories.
Adapted from Rogers (2003).

THE PROCESS OF INNOVATION

or necessity, for instance, having to get an e-mail account or a Twitter page for work.

The last category, which includes the final 16 percent of adopters, is the laggards. They "tend to be suspicious of innovations and of change agents."[10] Their deliberation process is "quite lengthy" and often driven by a precarious financial situation that makes purchasing a new product or changing the way that they do something very risky to them. Laggards want certainty before adopting something new.

Most hybrid homeschools are founded by innovators. Alison Morgan of the Classical Christian Conservatory of Alexandria, a hybrid program in the Washington, D.C., suburbs, described the initial families as a "rogue group." She said candidly that after it opened in 2017, the first year "was a rocky year for us, because there was no template. And so those were just really gracious, kind, patient families that came on and said, 'We are going to support this, because we see the need.'"

As she put it, being a founding family in a start-up hybrid homeschool is "not for the faint hearted." It takes a certain type of family to be willing to make the leap to a new school with an unfamiliar school model. Similarly, Martha Herndon of the Capitol Hill Learning Group, a cooperative preschool and hybrid micro-school where students attend small-group classes for three half-days each week, described the first families at the school as having a "pioneering spirit." They came to the school with an attitude of, "Hey, we've all got to work together to make this happen."

As Rogers argues, the total number of people who are willing to participate in a rogue group with a pioneering spirit is small. For hybrid homeschools to grow, they have to move into the realm of early adopters. How do they do that?

Attracting early adopters is about quelling fears. Early adopters are willing to take chances, but they need a bit more certainty than innovators do. They want to see some evidence of success. Herndon describes the growth and change at Capitol Hill Learning Group like this:

> I think that we had already built a community, because those people who went on into the kindergartens had already been here for preschool, we had already built a community, and it's a cooperative preschool, so we had already learned how to work together to make something happen. We had a teacher who was already at the school who was willing to teach the kindergarten class, so people knew her, so that helped.

Community is key. Rogers emphasizes the role of opinion leaders and communication networks in diffusing innovations. Communication networks are "interconnected individuals who are linked by patterned flows of information."[11] These are often rooted in like-minded groups; as Rogers writes, "Individuals tend to be linked to others who are close to them in physical distance and who are relatively homophilous in social characteristics."[12] People look to their friends and relatives to find out about new schools. They make connections at church and in their neighborhoods. Increasingly, social media creates platforms for groups of parents to share information about schools.

Communication networks and opinion leaders worked to diffuse information about hybrid homeschools and convinced early adopters to give them a try. One parent from a hybrid homeschool in the Washington, D.C., suburbs described how she learned about the school at church:

> My mom was visiting and we were at church, and she just happened to be talking to one of my friends. They were chatting about our son finishing elementary, that it was time for middle school, and that we wanted to do something different. . . . She didn't call it hybrid. She just said you go three days or two. . . . So my mom told me immediately, and we looked the information up. It happened that there was going to be one more open house that exact week.

A group of parents at a different D.C.-area hybrid homeschool recalled hearing about the program through an informal playgroup it arranged for preschool-age children and their caregivers. One mother struck up a conversation with "someone at the park," and that person "told us there was a preschool and so we went to the playgroup." Another mother found the playgroup, which led to the school, through the internet. "Back in 2010, I was lonely, I had no friends, I had one baby girl," she said. "And I was like, what do I do? So I typed in playgroups on the Hill, and [the school] came up."

At the Augustine Academy in Wisconsin, several communication networks connected families with the school. One parent said, "We lived in the same neighborhood as [one of the founding families], so we were their neighbors." Another said, "[My wife] got an e-mail from our sister-in-law about TAA. So, I think that that was one of the early ways that they got the word out, was kind of through the homeschool networks." Another parent mentioned local homeschooling networks. "For me, the Waukesha County Christian Home Educators was the group that we had been involved with," that parent said. "So, that was the platform that I saw the first piece of information about the school."

Social media plays a role as well in creating a communication network. As one parent commented,

We saw something on Facebook, and it was five minutes from our house. I had been homeschooling full-time at the time and not really looking. Then we were like, "Well, let's just go check it out. It's five minutes away," and we fell in love with it immediately. Yeah, it was a Facebook post.

These conversations also revealed the strong role played by opinion leadership, which is the "degree to which an individual is able to influence other individuals' attitudes or overt behavior informally in a desired way with relative frequency."[13] In speaking with hybrid homeschoolers, several different types of opinion leaders emerged. For instance, one hybrid homeschooling mother in Oklahoma was a speech language pathologist. When her clients shared challenges with their local schools, she would describe the hybrid program her son attended and offer it as a potential solution to the problems they were facing.

In addition, many families found out about schools at church, so clergy, board members, Bible study leaders, and committee members were important conduits of information. As one teacher in Wisconsin told me,

My Bible study leader, the woman who leads the Bible study I attend, said, "Stay after. I've got to tell you about this little school." I went, "I bet I know what you're going to mention." So, as it turned out, the [founding families] and our family all attended the same church, but because I have teenagers and they have youngers, we really hadn't intermixed. I mean, I kind of knew them by sight but hadn't really engaged in talking with them. So, then I started conversations. I think a week later I was hired as the kindergarten teacher.

Once schools are able to establish some key elements, they are in a much better place to answer the questions of more skeptical families. Having the same teacher, for example, allows new families to ask current families about the teacher that their child is going to have. Existing families can speak directly to his or her strengths and weaknesses.

Moving from serving innovators to early adopters presents new opportunities, but new challenges arise, too. Early adopters have less tolerance for bugs and will have stronger opinions about the types of things that they want to see in a school. The problems that they want to solve may be different, as well. Schools need to be careful as they extend their communities to take in new members. If founders want their school to retain its identity or key features, they will have to work hard to articulate its vision, philosophy, and how the school works. If that is not clear, they risk admitting families who will undermine what they are trying to do.

As Martha Herndon of Capitol Hill Learning Group put it,

> When we became a little bit more established, I started to notice that people were—and this is just human nature—that there was some complaining and things like that that didn't really happen at the beginning. . . . Later on, it was like, "I don't know if I like this and that, and I want to shift this." Learning how to be able to listen and hear what parents want, but at the same time know that there was a specific thing that I was going for with the school and wanted to stick by those foundational things. Because there was a time when people, I think, maybe would have shifted to, "Let's just do a full-day school," and that wasn't my vision. I didn't want that.

Even if hybrid homeschooling is able to capture a set of innovators and early adopters, these two groups still make up only a fraction of the total population. Can hybrid homeschooling break out from beyond these categories?

CROSSING THE CHASM AND THE WHOLE-PRODUCT PROBLEM

In 1991, Geoffrey Moore published *Crossing the Chasm*, a book about how new technologies get adopted. It would go on to become a massive international bestseller, selling more than 1 million print copies worldwide.

The "chasm" refers to the gap between the early adopters and the early majority from Rogers's classifications (consider Moore's subtitle: *Marketing and Selling Disruptive Products to Mainstream Customers*). As we have already discussed, the early majority is different from the two groups that precede it. Those in the early majority are more likely to be risk-averse and are not as impressed by new things. They just want things that work. As Moore says, "They want evolution, not revolution . . . and above all, they do not want to debug someone else's product."[14] To attract this group, products must solve a problem in a way that consumers are comfortable adopting.

What makes a solution comfortable for the early majority? One way of thinking about this is separating innovations into two types: continuous and disruptive. Continuous innovations make marginal improvements on existing technologies, like gasoline-powered cars with better fuel efficiency or personal computers with faster processing power. Disruptive technologies, on the other hand, cause us to change our behavior or the products that we use. Think of ride-sharing through a smartphone application, Lasik eye surgery instead of glasses, or using Spotify to listen to music instead of buying albums.

It is easier to sell the early and late majorities on continuous changes than disruptive ones. Continuous innovations have an easier time "crossing the chasm." But disruptive innovations can cross the chasm, too—so long as they know where to find their adopters.

So where does hybrid homeschooling fall? There are arguments to be made for either category, and different schools and school models may answer this question differently. Some will see themselves as a natural continuation of the experimentation and change that has, little by little, changed schools throughout time. They will market themselves to families that are looking to improve on what they are already doing, not completely change it.

Others will market themselves as disruptive, offering families a drastic change to help them overcome a serious problem. According to Moore, that strategy can help "cross the chasm" as well. Many families have vague or minor issues—they might not like their child's math teacher, or they might think that the way their child is taught reading is suboptimal. There are solutions to these problems that are less disruptive than taking 50 percent of their child's education into their own hands—families can choose a different school or participate in such after-school supplemental activities as enrichment clubs or tutoring.

But a small but substantial number of families have problems with the traditional school model that are more fundamental. As we learned earlier, some parents believe deeply that the contemporary school schedule and calendar are out of step with the rhythms of family life. They cite school programs that do not meet their child's needs and a culture of overscheduling and homework that isolates children from their parents during important times of development. They want to radically disrupt their child's days, weeks, and years.

For these families, hybrid homeschooling, disruptive though it may be, can be a solution. It can also be a solution for families who have serious, foundational disagreements with the pedagogical or moral philosophies of their local public or private schools, either because they are more or less progressive, conservative, or religious. It is not surprising that there are hybrid homeschools organized around both the Waldorf and classical models.

There is one more thing that can help hybrid homeschools "cross the chasm." It is tied to what Moore calls the "whole-product" concept. Because products can almost never fully live up to the promises of salespeople or the expectations of consumers, innovators must augment their products with services and supplementary tools that make it do everything that consumers want it to do. Think about all of the apps on a smartphone that allow it to fulfill its full potential.

Hybrid homeschooling has a whole-product problem. That is, for a hybrid homeschool to work, it needs additional services and supplementary elements. These include a curriculum designed to maximize the potential of the homeschool model, professional development resources tuned to the unique needs of hybrid teachers, and tools to communicate with parents, who play a much larger role than in traditional schools. Hybrid homeschools also need schedules, policies, and all the typical resources that help a school function that are aligned with the unique needs of their model.

So how can schools work through the whole-product problem? A few things can happen. First, curriculum and professional development providers can recognize hybrid homeschools as an emerging market. As more parents choose hybrid homeschools, there is more opportunity for organizations that create curriculum and professional development to serve them. In interviews, homeschool leaders voiced frustration with adapting existing curricula for a hybrid model. And because many teachers are from nontraditional backgrounds and preparation paths, they have a unique set of needs that professional development providers could help meet.

Second, more hybrid homeschools can formally or informally connect with one another to share expertise and resources. Some hybrid programs already do this; for example, the network of more than 80 university-model schools share information and common resources. Hybrid homeschools that follow established programs, for example, Charlotte Mason or Waldorf, do as well. As a parent at the Augustine Academy stated,

> For every start-up, your thought process is always, "Okay, this is a start-up. These are new ideas. There's going to be a lot of growing pains." Whenever you look at a start-up, you're concerned. I think for us what solidified is, you have Ambleside, which provides all of the training, the materials, the method, the curriculum. So, it's already established, and we are just an extension basically of what they were already doing around the world.

Ambleside filled out the offerings of the school according to Charlotte Mason's model, providing a coherent curriculum, professional development resources, and even videos for prospective parents to understand how the model works and its benefits.

Networking could also help hybrid homeschools that are not connected to an established model and want to retain their individuality. Through the internet, schools can create more formal relationships with one another to pool purchasing and back-office support, further driving down the cost of providing education to their students. Software licenses, curriculum materials, hardware, and a host of other resources are cheaper when bought in bulk, and schools working together to make purchasing decisions could be a huge boon. Such networks might also help schools launch and scale more smoothly, because founders won't have to discover and invent each of the logistical processes necessary to deliver group instruction. This could also help win over the early majority, who are looking for a smoother experience and are less willing to put up with bugs.

Third, philanthropic organizations can bridge the gaps. Numerous organizations are dedicated to seeding and scaling new schools and new ventures in education, for instance, the NewSchools Venture Fund, the Drexel Fund, 4.0 Schools, LeanLab Education, and the Charter School Growth Fund, among others. These philanthropies and incubators try to identify promising schools or education ventures, help them solve problems, and work toward financial stability and expansion. They can lend technical assistance to hybrid homeschools as well. Each of these organizations has its own priorities and kinds of schools it supports, but chances are, there is a hybrid homeschool or potential hybrid homeschool that would align with their missions.

TWO LESSONS

Pulling these strands together, what can hybrid homeschooling tell us about innovation in education? There are two key lessons. First, *start with people and their problems*. Too frequently, educational innovators start with a solution and then start looking for a problem for it to solve. Entrepreneurs hack some technological innovation and see that it could have implications for schools, so they go around trying to convince educators that it will make their lives better. Policy advocates see a successful program in one school or district and then try and get other schools or districts to adopt it. In both cases, the innovation may or may not be a good fit, but they push it anyway.

Hybrid homeschooling points to a different solution. In almost every case, these schools were founded by people trying to solve specific problems that they themselves were experiencing. After starting the school, they found other parents and students with the same challenge, and through word of mouth, these schools started to grow. Demand has been driven almost entirely by individual families seeking models that meet their particular needs, not through outreach or marketing.

That's why these programs look different based on the problems that they are trying to solve. The public hybrid homeschools in California that serve students pushed out by the traditional system look different from the private religious hybrid homeschools within the Dallas–Fort Worth metroplex in Texas. Hybrid homeschooling is a broad umbrella that lots of different educators with different philosophies and offerings can use to tailor education to the communities that they serve.

The second lesson has to do with choosing the right battles. Hybrid homeschools *focus on solving a small number of major problems, rather than taking on a broad range of secondary needs*. Traditionally, education has not done this. Schools have been designed to maximize the number of students who attend them and try and do pretty well for all of them. Think of how most state accountability systems work. Schools are judged based on average student performance. As long as enough positives wash out the negatives, schools are deemed effective. Hybrid homeschools take the opposite approach. They freely admit that they aren't for everyone and are laser-focused on a group of people and the problems that they have.

These typically include families who want a private, religious, or particular pedagogical education for their children but cannot afford it. They are dissatisfied with their local public offerings, often bringing with them terrible stories of their children's suffering in those schools. This is an intense problem that private hybrid homeschools and many charter hybrid homeschools solve. Whether it is the project-based learning of Da Vinci Connect in Los Angeles or the Waldorf model of the Mountain Phoenix Community School in the Denver suburbs, families who have strong beliefs about the type of education that their child should receive can access that for free.

A second set of problems involves families of children with unique physical, cognitive, and emotional needs. These students often do not find traditional schools to be a place where they can thrive, and some families have found the personalized flexibility of hybrid homeschools to be a more nurturing and educationally rich environment for their children. Watching a child suffer can be agonizing for parents, and striking the right educational balance is paramount. In talking to these families, the relief in their voices is clear. It is as if a millstone has been taken off their shoulders. They are happy, they are grateful, and they can move on with their lives.

Finally, some families hate the workings of traditional schools and refuse to let those rhythms dictate their lives. This applies to families of all stripes, those whose religious faith takes precedence over school schedules, those who are devoted to child-led, experiential learning, and those who just want their kids back. Hybrid homeschools give these diverse families the "gift of time." They put them primarily in charge of what, when, and how children learn.

These are important lessons that educators should take to heart. By starting with people and their problems, working to deeply understand their issues and motivations, and thinking through how families will use a school to make their and their children's lives better, schools can be more responsive to particular needs—and ultimately more effective.

NOTES

1. "Entrepreneurship." *Economist*, April 27, 2009, https://www.economist.com/news/2009/04/27/entrepreneurship (accessed October 21, 2020).

2. Mitchell Stevens, *Kingdom of Children: Culture and Controversy in the Homeschooling Movement*. Princeton, N.J.: Princeton University Press, 2001, 6.

3. Rikke Friis Dam and Teo Yu Siang, "What Is Design Thinking and Why Is It So Popular?" *Interation-Design.org*, July 20, 2020, https://www.interaction-design.org/literature/article/what-is-design-thinking-and-why-is-it-so-popular (accessed October 21, 2020).

4. Jeanne Liedtka, "Why Design Thinking Works." *Harvard Business Review*, September/October 2018, https://hbr.org/2018/09/why-design-thinking-works (accessed October 21, 2020).

5. Everett M. Rogers, *Diffusion of Innovations*. New York: Free Press, 2003.

6. Rogers, *Diffusion of Innovations*, 283.

7. Rogers, *Diffusion of Innovations*, 283.

8. Rogers, *Diffusion of Innovations*, 284.

9. Rogers, *Diffusion of Innovations*, 284.

10. Rogers, *Diffusion of Innovations*, 284.

11. Rogers, *Diffusion of Innovations*, 337.

12. Rogers, *Diffusion of Innovations*, 341.

13. Rogers, *Diffusion of Innovations*, 27.

14. Geoffrey A. Moore, *Crossing the Chasm: Marketing and Selling Disruptive Products to Mainstream Customers*. New York: HarperBusiness, 2006, 26.

CONCLUSION

Michelle Rainey is both a parent and the principal at Da Vinci Connect High School, a hybrid homeschool charter in Los Angeles. Her account of the school's genesis and goals echoes the sentiments, conversations, and lessons of this volume.

> And so the idea came to serve homeschoolers and to give them something different. There's independent study schools, there's charters filling out the affidavit and going off the grid, but for homeschoolers that also want a school-based experience, there's less. We thought it would be this small school that not very many people would be all that interested in. . . . Our wait lists were huge, even bigger and more competitive than our five-day high school program, which really kind of astounded everyone.

She went on to say,

> I think they really thought like, "You believe the myths of homeschooling and who it's for. And it's for these really conservative families that are all wearing matching polos, sitting around the dining room table, studying together." And that's not why people are choosing homeschooling or hybrid schooling. It's not who we're serving in majority. . . . What we're really trying to do in the grand scale is challenge what we believe about how kids learn and the opportunities that we give them, and take that to a different place.

As this book comes in for a landing, it is worth taking a moment to draw together some summarizing thoughts. Is this a phenomenon that is going to grow? If so, who are the likely people to populate these schools? Even if hybrid homeschooling doesn't grow, are there lessons that hybrid homeschools can teach us about education writ large? If so, what are they?

Rainey's words point to the answer to the first question. Hybrid homeschools throughout the country fill quickly and frequently have waiting lists. That tells us that more families are interested than are currently served. Exactly how many is unclear, but the demand is there. As for who will take advantage of this school model—that's an interesting question, and one worth dwelling on.

WHO IS HYBRID HOMESCHOOLING FOR?

Over and over, both parents and educators from hybrid homeschools have said that their schools are "not for everyone." It is worth thinking about who might benefit from hybrid homeschooling and who might not.

In *Crossing the Chasm*, Geoffrey Moore recommends that purveyors of new technologies create libraries of "customer characterizations," profiles of potential users of their technology. Innovators should ask such questions as the following: Who might use our product? How might they use it? What problems do they need to have solved?

Following this advice, who might the potential users of the hybrid homeschool model be? What problems would motivate them, and how would they use hybrid homeschooling as a solution?

Let's look at four potential customer types, based on both on the preceding interviews and a close look at homeschooling trends in general: *the underestimated child of color*, *the urban Christian*, *the kid who needs a break*, and *the middle-income pedagogue*.

The Underestimated Child of Color

Many parents of black, Hispanic, and Asian children worry that schools do not recognize or respect their child's full potential. They have good reason to think this. Researchers Nicholas Papageorge, Seth Gershenson, and Kyung Min Kang analyzed data from the Educational Longitudinal Survey of 2002, and found that white teachers, who account for 79 percent of all U.S. public school teachers, have far lower expectations for black students than they do for similarly situated white students.[1] Some families of color

CONCLUSION

also may want to teach their children particular culture and traditions, and traditional public schools (and even many private schools) are not always interested in helping. As mentioned in chapter 1, these reasons, and more, have been driving more and more minority families to homeschool.

Hybrid homeschooling presents a solution to a very clear problem for these families. It is parent-directed, so they can make sure that their child's talents and abilities are affirmed. And they can pass down the values, culture, and traditions that they cherish. But the work is not entirely on their shoulders. For a relatively low cost, or for no cost, if the option is public, parents can collaborate with trained educators to fill the gaps in their skills or confidence. Their child can have both an affirming and academically rigorous education.

The Urban Christian

American culture is secularizing. According to the Pew Research Center's Forum on Religion and Public Life, the percentage of Americans who identify as Christian declined by 12 percentage points from 2009 to 2019, to a new low of 65 percent, while the number of Americans who identify as religiously unaffiliated increased by 9 percentage points in the same time period, to 26 percent.[2] Schools sit downstream from this cultural phenomenon. They reflect the dominant culture. And that makes them increasingly likely to promote ideas about gender, sexuality, and right and wrong that are at odds with some orthodox Christian teachings. These forces are most at play in U.S. cities, which for decades have been found to be less religious, on average, than rural and suburban communities.[3]

At the same time, opportunity is clustering in cities. This can put many young, educated Christians in a bind. To have good career and economic opportunities, they typically need to live in places that can be hostile toward their values. Each day, unless they can afford private school or are able to homeschool on a full-time basis, they must send their children to public schools whose teachings may contradict what they believe. Many of these urban religious families will be looking for a refuge, for local schools that reflect and teach their values, but at a reasonable cost.

Hybrid homeschools would seem a great option for them. A full-time religious private school might be out of their reach, but the lower tuition rate of a hybrid school could be within their budget. In addition, teaching homeschool on a full-time schedule might be daunting as well, and a hybrid model can lighten that workload. These families also would benefit from joining a like-minded community, organized according to not only the religious character of the school, but also the shared experience of hybrid homeschooling.

The Kid Who Needs a Break

Many of the families interviewed for this book believe that schools do not match the developmental needs and rhythms of growing children. School schedules plus extracurricular activities and homework can crowd out quality time with parents. Schools also can be breeding grounds for negative social dynamics like bullying—both in person and online—which schools are often powerless to stop.

In addition, as mentioned in chapter 3, diagnoses of anxiety and depression in children are on the rise.[4] The exact causes are unclear, but parents attribute some of these issues to the overall culture of schooling. Many students find traditional school environments overwhelming. Students with sensory processing disorders or anxiety can get thrown out of whack by seemingly innocuous interactions or classroom stimuli. Students with executive-functioning challenges can get frustrated by lockstep group lessons. The COVID-19 pandemic has generated a fair amount of stress and anxiety in parents as well.

Hybrid homeschooling changes the rhythm of schooling and the environment that children learn in. Parents can provide more support and flexibility, and have more opportunities to manage how their child interacts with the outside environment. This cuts both ways: Parents can offer more protection and direct supervision to children who need it, and other parents can allow their children more independence and more opportunities to take risks than a traditional school would. They can get the benefits of a traditional school environment and the socialization that comes with it without being overwhelmed by it. And for kids who struggle to attend school at all, extra time at home can be crucial. Sometimes, knowing that they don't have to go back tomorrow can be a powerful tool to get things back on track after a rough day.

The Middle-Income Pedagogues

Many families are drawn to particular pedagogical philosophies. Waldorf education typically appeals to more progressive families because it places the student at the center of education in a journey of discovery and exploration. Project-based learning appeals to families that want their children

CONCLUSION

doing practical work and learning via real-world tasks. Classical education appeals to parents who want their children to read the great books and tap into wells of knowledge dug by some of humanity's greatest thinkers.

Most schools with these pedagogical orientations are private and expensive. This mismatch between families' educational goals and ability to pay within current systems creates an opportunity for alternative education models to take root. Hybrid homeschools like the Mountain Phoenix Community School (a Waldorf school), Da Vinci Connect (a project-based learning school), the Augustine Academy (an Ambleside school), Legacy Classical Christian Academy (a classical school), and others profiled here can help meet that need.

In addition, the challenges in returning to traditional, full-time schooling in the wake of COVID-19 are prompting some families to think differently about how to make school happen—including in ways that meet their pedagogical desires at a price that they can afford.

WHO IS HYBRID HOMESCHOOLING NOT FOR?

Hybrid homeschooling is not a solution for every family or every school in the United States. As has been made clear by the coronavirus pandemic, many families need schools to not only educate their children, but also keep them safe and occupied for as much of the work week as possible. Low-income families rely on schools to provide meals and other social services to their children. Families with children with special needs count on daily school schedules to provide predictability, regular opportunities to socialize, and specialized therapies and activities that parents can't provide at home. Full-time school works best to meet these needs.

There are also lots of parents who are satisfied with their existing school options. In the *2019 Schooling in America Survey*, my colleagues, Paul DiPerna, Andrew Catt, and Michael Shaw, found fairly broad approval. Looking at parent opinions by school type, they found that 75 percent of private-school parents gave their school an "A" or "B" grade, compared to 61 percent of charter-school parents and 48 percent of public-school parents.[5] Even the relatively small share of 48 percent of public-school parents represents a huge number of people. Those folks are happy with their options and probably aren't interested in trying something different.

The sort of teaching that hybrid homeschooling requires is most certainly not for every teacher—plenty would hate it. Working hand-in-glove with parents can be time-consuming and annoying for teachers who have a specific vision of what they want their classroom to look like and what they want their students to accomplish. A nontrivial number of teachers get offended when parents question their professional judgment. This is not a model for them.

Many teachers also cannot take the financial hit of part-time employment. It is true that many public and public charter hybrid homeschooling models find ways to give teachers a full teaching load and thus a full teaching salary, but not every school can. If the teacher does not have a partner with a substantial enough income or a part-time job to help bridge the gap, they cannot make it work.

LESSONS

The idiosyncratic nature of hybrid homeschools means that they aren't for everyone. But the preconditions that allow them to thrive are universal. These stories offer accessible lessons for all.

In founding or joining a hybrid homeschool, families identify what educational goals and experiences are important to them and determine what they can do to bring that vision to life. They are highly focused in this effort, and their example provides three particular lessons for any school leader. First, hybrid homeschooling solves the intense problems of a small number of people instead of the minor problems of a lot of people. Second, hybrid homeschools foster community and connection in a time of alienation and atomization. Third, hybrid homeschools make better use of the most precious resource we have: time.

Solving Intense Problems

A parent who feels that their child with special needs is being ignored, neglected, or forgotten can think of nothing else. It is tough to work. It is tough to sleep. It is tough to go on living a normal life. Similarly, a parent who feels that their child is being taught things that are morally wrong or that will lead them to be an immoral person can be torn apart by worry. Parents who believe that school environments are subjecting their children to bullying or stifling their creativity can be consumed by guilt. And families who feel pulled apart by schedules that don't work for them or hours of homework and activities that encroach on quality time together may fear that they are ruining days, months, and years of their children's childhoods.

CONCLUSION

These are intense problems. This is not, "I'm angry my kid didn't make the cheerleading squad." When schools challenge fundamental aspects of families' values or lives together, we find deep, existential crises for parents.

Hybrid homeschools set out to solve these problems. The goal is to give parents time back with their children. The founders want to provide pedagogical environments that parents believe are best for their children at prices that they can afford. They want to create safe, nurturing environments for students with special needs. If a parent has one of these problems, the schools are intent on solving them.

The education system can learn from this. School leaders should ask themselves the following: What are the intense problems of the families in our community? What are the two or three biggest challenges that people face, and how can we solve them? The answers will vary widely, given the vast diversity of communities in the United States. But by starting with these questions, schools and school districts can be more focused and more successful. Rather than worrying about solving every little problem that crops up and getting bogged down in bureaucratic minutiae, leaders of any type of school can prioritize, direct their energies where they will matter most, and address families' most pressing needs. Schools focused on the big things will strengthen communities, increase support for schools, and create institutions that get things done.

Fostering Community and Connection

In his brilliant 2019 book *Alienated America: Why Some Places Thrive While Others Collapse*, Tim Carney argues that the American Dream is thought to be dead because "strong communities have crumbled, and much of America has been left abandoned, without the web of human connections and institutions that make the good life possible."[6] And, as mentioned earlier, Yuval Levin's 2020 book *A Time to Build* argues that we need "devotion to the work that we do with others in the service of a common aspiration, and therefore devotion to the institutions we compose and inhabit."[7]

Schools are important institutions. They are communities. They connect us to one another and allow us to work together toward the common goal of educating our children. They form and shape the children that attend them, and as we have seen, they can also form and shape the parents of those children as well.

For too long, schools have alienated parents. As traditional schools professionalized throughout the course of the twentieth century, education began to be seen as the purview of experts. Too many schools essentially told parents, "Just put your child on the bus, we'll take it from there." This drove a wedge between parents and teachers, and what was formerly seen as a shared enterprise between the adults in a community became a distant, or even adversarial, relationship between trained educators and untrained parents. Today, even schools that profess to value parent involvement often make it difficult for parents to ask hard questions or participate in the classroom. Instead, they steer families' enthusiasm and support toward parent–teacher association committee meetings, holiday parties, and annual "back-to-school" night presentations. This cannot continue. Families and schools have to work together. The task they share is too difficult and too important.

So how can schools get better at fostering community? The first step is a change in attitude. Educators need to see parents not as an annoyance or an uneducated, self-interested mob, but rather as partners in children's education. That said, if educators see parents as partners, parents need to act like it. They need to be more helpful to teachers and less adversarial with them.

The second change is the actual work of schools. Hybrid homeschools present a unique opportunity for families with similar views about child-rearing, child psychology, morality, religion, and a host of other affinities to create institutions together. This binds them together in common cause and helps channel their energies into something productive. Traditional schools need to find similar opportunities to articulate what shared vision or values animate their work and use that vision to influence school culture and build a stronger school community.

The best way to do this is to make education less centralized and less hierarchical. By allowing more school-level autonomy and promoting a pluralistic vision of what the education system can look like, schools with unique, coherent missions can grow and knit together communities in the process. Schools don't have to be hybrid homeschools to be tight-knit. They simply need a clear, shared purpose and the freedom to achieve it.

The third and final change is directed toward traditional public schools. Districts in Michigan, Kentucky, and California (and elsewhere) have found ways to work with, instead of against, homeschoolers. Rather than seeing homeschoolers as adversaries, superintendents like Brian Creasman in Fleming County recognized that homeschoolers are part of the same community as public schoolers and have needs that public schools can help solve. He listened. Homeschoolers responded in good faith, and together they have created a thriving program. Rather than undermine one another, they reinforce one another. In a world with so much social conflict, finding areas for rapprochement is important. Districts like Fleming County offer a way to achieve it.

CONCLUSION

Making Time Count

Hybrid homeschoolers have plenty of critiques of traditional schools, but perhaps the most stinging is that they waste a ton of time. Hybrid homeschoolers argue that they can get more done in fewer hours of the day and give students and families more free time. In their view, much of the work done in a structured and regimented way in school can be completed more quickly in a less structured, more flexible home environment.

School schedules can be difficult to change. Most individual schools operate within larger systems that share buses and sports fields, for example, which makes schedule predictability important. And family schedules orbit around school start and end times because that's when parents are able to leave the house to work. Staff expectations and negotiated contracts build on traditional calendars, with about six and a half hours of instruction on a typical day and breaks around typical holidays.

That said, just because schools have to fit a particular schedule does not mean that they have to waste the time that they are given. Schools could give students more free and flexible time in the school day. High schools could operate more like colleges, with students having blocks of time on campus that are free for them to use as they wish.

But on a more fundamental level, school leaders need to ask themselves these questions: How are students spending their time in school? Are schools really getting the most out of the limited time that they have? How many minutes and hours are wasted by pointless interruptions? Do administrative tasks rob classes of valuable instructional time? Do students' workloads expand or contract to fit the time allotted, or are assignments thoughtful extensions of what students need to learn and be able to do? Are students getting anything out of their homework, or are they just exhaustedly going through the motions? Do activities and sports fit within family calendars and schedules?

Time is a precious resource. Schools already have only a fraction of a student's day, week, month, and year. School leaders should question whether teachers and students are making the most of their time. If leaders are honest, many will realize that they are not.

THE FUTURE

Let's imagine a brighter future together. Let's look beyond alienation, frustration, and suspicion. Instead, imagine living in a country and world that is connected, compassionate, trusting, empathetic, and happy. A place where people feel rooted to communities. Where they believe in institutions. In such a world, people work with and within those institutions to both form themselves into better people and form their children into the types of adults they want them to be. They are civically engaged. They feel called to higher purpose. They are living good lives.

Hybrid homeschooling can help get us there. Oftentimes, critics worry that homeschoolers are atomistic and pursue a hyper-individualized vision that starts with opting out of community schools. This is a poor understanding of homeschooling, but setting that aside, it is the direct inverse of the hybrid homeschool vision.

Hybrid homeschoolers are countercultural, but they are not opting out of community. They are creating new communities and new institutions that bind them to one another and enrich the fabric of their lives. These schools can address the urgent needs of some families. They can put the limited time that families have to its best and highest use. And they can tackle the big, weighty, thorny, knotty problems that confront us.

The families and educators whose voices make up the bulk of this volume, and the schools that they have created, challenge the trends of the day. At a time when people are moving apart, hybrid homeschools are drawing people together. At a time when people seem to obsess about trivialities, they are asking big questions. At a time when people are retreating from a shared, common life, they are stepping forward. We can learn a lot from them.

We don't know how many hybrid homeschools there will be in 5, 10, or 20 years' time. But we do know that if the philosophies that animate them become more widespread, we just might make our world a better place.

NOTES

1. Nicholas Papageorge, Seth Gershenson, and Kyung Min Kang, "Teacher Expectations Matter," *National Bureau of Education Research*, working paper 25255, November 2018, https://www.nber.org/papers/w25255.pdf (accessed October 20, 2020).

2. Pew Research Center, "In U.S., Decline of Christianity Continues at Rapid Pace." *Pew Research Center*, October 17, 2019, https://www.pewforum.org/2019/10/17/in-u-s-decline-of-christianity-continues-at-rapid-pace/ (accessed October 20, 2020).

3. Linda Lyons, "Age, Religiosity, and Rural America." *Gallup*, March 11, 2003, https://news.gallup.com/poll/7960/age-religiosity-rural-america.aspx (accessed October 21, 2020).

4. Centers for Disease Control and Prevention, "Anxiety and Depression in Children: Get the Facts." *CDC.org*, https://www.cdc.gov/childrensmentalhealth/features/anxiety-depression-children.html (accessed October 21, 2020).

5. Paul DiPerna, Andrew D. Catt, and Michael Shaw, *2019 Schooling in America Survey: Public Opinion on K–12 Education, Busing, Technology, and School Choice*. Indianapolis, IN: EdChoice, 2019. Available at https://www.edchoice.org/wp-content/uploads/2019/10/2019-9-Schooling-in-America-by-Paul-Diperna-Andrew-Catt-and-Michael-Shaw-1.pdf (accessed October 20, 2020).

6. Timothy P. Carney, *Alienated America: Why Some Places Thrive While Others Collapse*. New York: HarperCollins, 2019, 13.

7. Yuval Levin, *A Time to Build: From Family and Community to Congress and the Campus, How Recommitting to Our Institutions Can Revive the American Dream*. New York: Basic Books, 2020, 202.

Appendix

SO YOU WANT TO HYBRID HOMESCHOOL?

If you've made it this far through the book and think hybrid homeschooling might be something you'd like to try, read on. This short appendix covers the key questions that potential hybrid homeschoolers should ask themselves and resources that are available to help.

Hybrid homeschooling is not easy, and it is not for the faint of heart. By answering these questions honestly and wrestling with their full implications, parents and teachers can set themselves up for success.

KEY QUESTIONS FOR PARENTS

Am I ready for the responsibility that comes with taking a larger stake in my child's education?

If you choose to hybrid homeschool, anywhere from one to four days of your child's school week will happen under your supervision. Are you ready to take over scheduling? Can you handle "classroom" management—i.e., keeping your child on task or, if you have multiple children, ensuring they are working instead of distracting one another? Are you prepared to lead instruction? You will need to establish a space for your children to learn and plan out days, weeks, and months of instruction. It is a substantial commitment. Are you ready?

Do I want to have a closer relationship with my child's teacher?

If you're used to a classroom newsletter once a month and a parent–teacher conference once or twice a year, strap in for a major change. Hybrid homeschooling teachers and parents have a constant line of communication, frequently calling or texting, chatting at pickup and drop-off, and exchanging lots of e-mails. In addition, parents often rely on teachers to demystify complex topics before they attempt to teach them at home. Are you ready to be that vulnerable? Can you admit what you do not know and need help with? Can you collaborate well? Are you willing to work with another adult in designing your child's education?

Do I want to blur the line between parent and teacher?

Parents frequently underestimate the shift in their relationships with their children when they step into a teaching role at home. "School" rules tend to be less flexible than family dynamics, and that can be a point of pressure for some homeschooling parents. If a child doesn't eat his dinner or says something mean to a sibling, a parent may choose to respond with a variety of repercussions and consequences based on a host of factors. But if a student doesn't do his math work, the consequences in terms of grading are clear, and the job of the teaching parent is to impose them. It's a lot of pressure, and some parents would prefer to leave that to educators outside of the home. When homeschooling works well, it fosters an incredibly close relationship between parent and child. They learn and grow together in ways that are not possible when a child is enrolled in a traditional school. But when it doesn't work, it can sour both home and school life.

Do I have the financial flexibility to give up my job or to work part-time?

Depending on the model, parents will need to commit several days each week to focused teaching work. That requires either a flexible work schedule or a home budget that can accommodate one parent not working. It is important to look at both sides of the ledger, since hybrid homeschools are relatively inexpensive, which might decrease the need for additional income. But a full accounting is necessary before undertaking hybrid homeschooling.

Am I ready to commit to a school community that might ask more of me than other schools?

Hybrid homeschooling communities tend to be tight-knit entities. Many schools expect parents to volunteer and be part of the broader school community. This can be a powerful and positive experience, but it is a commitment. Are you an introvert? Do you want to be left alone? Entering into a close community might not be for you. But you never know how you might benefit from getting drawn into a group.

Is this the right environment for my child?

This is perhaps the hardest question. Parents need to ask what is missing from their child's education and whether this new model can provide it. Maybe it can, maybe it can't.

KEY QUESTIONS FOR EDUCATORS

Do I want to answer to parents more than I would in a traditional school?

In any school, teachers count on parents to support learning at home, by helping with science projects, sewing play costumes, or forcing reluctant students to do their homework. But when parents get *too* involved, when they ask tough questions or have an opinion about a subject or assignment, teachers often dismiss them as self-centered, tactless, and annoying.

Because teachers trust their training and skills, some just wish parents would drop the questions and trust them as well. A hybrid homeschool probably isn't for them. Teachers in hybrid homeschools frequently communicate with parents and are expected to take feedback charitably. When this back-and-forth works well, it can lead to a much more hospitable environment for teaching and learning, as children realize that their parents and teachers are on the same team and it's in their best interest to get with the program. But it takes the right personalities to make that work.

Do I want to work with parents, educating them in areas where they struggle?

Teachers in hybrid homeschools have to help parents, as well as students. Parents don't always understand what they are supposed to be teaching their children, so teachers need to be comfortable answering such e-mails or phone calls as, "I'm supposed to be teaching sentence diagramming, but I'm not sure how to classify a predicate nominative." Teaching adults is different than teaching children. Adults are used to having the answers, so teachers need to be willing to walk through the process of learning with them. Teachers also need to explain pedagogical philosophy to parents and prescribe how a particular activity fits a Montessori or classical education, for example. They have to be confident enough in their understanding of the ethos of the school to help parents understand it.

Am I willing to take a pay cut?

Full-time teaching salaries can be hard to come by, particularly in private hybrid homeschools. The flexibility of the model and smaller paycheck may work for retired teachers or teachers who are raising a family or have a spouse with a substantial source of income. But for financially independent teachers, particularly young teachers, the salary situation can be a challenge.

Can I make the schedule work with other sources of income?

Many teachers in hybrid homeschools stitch together multiple income streams to earn a necessary wage. With a growing number of flexible options for employment, for instance, substitute teaching, dog sitting, or driving for a rideshare company, these "side hustles" could be used to make teaching at a hybrid homeschool work for teachers who really want the job.

Do I want to move faster than at a typical school?

Hybrid homeschool classrooms do not waste time. That puts pressure on teachers to be ready to move quickly through a lot of content. It takes planning and preparation. The upside is that teachers who love their subject can cover a lot of it, and quickly. But the downside is that teachers need to be ready for a faster pace during their limited face-to-face time with their students. Unfortunately, curriculum and other resources for hybrid homeschool teachers are limited, so it's on individual teachers to develop lessons and classroom practices that accommodate a hybrid schedule. This is an additional burden.

RESOURCES

Resources for hybrid homeschoolers have grown in the past few years, with like-minded families finding one another on social media and parents seeking out creative solutions to the challenges posed by the COVID-19 pandemic. Below are some well-regarded resources from a variety of sources, both for families looking to start hybrid homeschools and parents who want to enroll a child in an existing school.

Carol Topp, the Homeschool CPA (www.homeschoolcpa.com)

This website offers a ton of resources on legal compliance, tax status, and best practices for parents and those hoping to open schools. It offers sample bylaws, articles of incorporation, reimbursement forms, and a host of other key documents. Topp also offers consulting services directly to prospective and current school operators.

The Colorado Department of Education (https://www.cde.state.co.us/choice/homeschool_resources)

A state education agency's website might not be the first place one would think to go to find homeschooling information, but Colorado's Department of Education has curated a great set of resources for both Colorado families and homeschoolers in general. It has links to specific programs available in public schools in Colorado, as well as private homeschooling support groups and education providers geared toward homeschooling families.

Hillsdale College Homeschool at Home (https://k12athome.hillsdale.edu/)

For those interested in classical curriculum, Michigan's Hillsdale College has a wealth of resources, including an online program for K–12 students, available on its website, along with an active blog with resources and reflections of classical and home educators.

Homeschool Legal Defense Association (www.hslda.org)

HSLDA is the largest organization of homeschool families in the country. It advocates for homeschoolers and provides legal support for homeschooling families. It is the go-to resource for the latest updates on homeschooling laws and can be a resource for families with specific questions about the legality of their schooling arrangements.

University Model Schools International (www.umsi.org)

The umbrella organization for university-model hybrid homeschools, UMSI's website offers a wealth of resources for parents and potential school operators. UMSI offers new-school development workshops, provides detailed plans for families and educators hoping to start a university-model school, and hosts regional and national events for representatives of university-model schools.

BIBLIOGRAPHY

Bartholet, Elizabeth. "Homeschooling: Parent Rights Absolutism vs. Child Rights to Education and Protection." *Arizona Law Review* 62, no. 1 (2020): 1–80.

California Charter Schools Association. "A Summary of AB 1505 and AB 1507." *Hubspot .net*, https://cdn2.hubspot.net/hubfs/3049635/AB%201505_1507%20Brief.pdf ?__hssc=206422988.1.1590069663186&__hstc=206422988.b4d7fc4011ed8f1 b0ccb23dd7f559dfa.1590069663185.1590069663185.1590069663185.1&__hsfp =946197843&hsCtaTracking=7b7ef75f-12f1-485d-a697-34ff26e21f67%7C8 b85d1ef-73ba-4e81-9dbd-aca65d956fc8 (accessed October 20, 2020).

Carney, Timothy P. *Alienated America: Why Some Places Thrive While Others Collapse.* New York: HarperCollins, 2019.

Centers for Disease Control and Prevention. "Anxiety and Depression in Children: Get the Facts." *CDC.org*, https://www.cdc.gov/childrensmentalhealth/features/ anxiety-depression-children.html (accessed October 21, 2020).

Chiodo, Abbigail J., Ruben Hernandez-Murillo, and Michael T. Owyang. "Nonlinear Effects of School Quality on House Prices." *Federal Reserve Bank of St. Louis Review* 92, no. 3 (May/June 2010): 185–204.

Dam, Rikke Friis, and Teo Yu Siang. "What Is Design Thinking and Why Is It So Popular?" *Interation-Design.org*, July 20, 2020, at https://www.interaction -design.org/literature/article/what-is-design-thinking-and-why-is-it-so-popular (accessed July 20, 2020).

Denizet-Lewis, Benoit. "Why Are More American Teenagers Than Ever Suffering from Severe Anxiety?" *New York Times Magazine*, October 11, 2017, https:// www.nytimes.com/2017/10/11/magazine/why-are-more-american-teenagers -than-ever-suffering-from-severe-anxiety.html (accessed May 19, 2020).

DiPerna, Paul, and Michael Shaw. *2018 Schooling in America Survey: Public Opinion on K–12 Education, Parent and Teacher Experiences, Accountability, and School Choice.* Indianapolis, IN: EdChoice, 2018. Available at https://www.edchoice.org/wp-content/uploads/2018/12/2018-12-Schooling-In-America-by-Paul-DiPerna-and-Michael-Shaw.pdf (accessed May 19, 2020).

DiPerna, Paul, Andrew D. Catt, and Michael Shaw. *2019 Schooling in America Survey: Public Opinion on K–12 Education, Busing, Technology, and School Choice.* Indianapolis, IN: EdChoice, 2019. Available at https://www.edchoice.org/wp-content/uploads/2019/10/2019-9-Schooling-in-America-by-Paul-DiPerna-Andrew-Catt-and-Michael-Shaw-1.pdf (accessed October 20, 2020).

Douglas, Dianna. "Are Private Schools Immoral?" *Atlantic*, December 14, 2017, https://www.theatlantic.com/education/archive/2017/12/progressives-are-undermining-public-schools/548084/ (accessed October 21, 2020).

Dwyer, James G., and Shawn F. Peters. *Homeschooling: The History and Philosophy of a Controversial Practice.* Chicago: University of Chicago Press, 2019.

EdChoice. "The ABCs of School Choice: 2020 Edition." *EdChoice.org*, January 22, 2020, https://www.edchoice.org/research/the-abcs-of-school-choice/ (accessed October 20, 2020).

"Entrepreneurship." *Economist*, April 27, 2009, https://www.economist.com/news/2009/04/27/entrepreneurship (accessed October 21, 2020).

Fields-Smith, Cheryl, and Monica Wells Kisura. "Resisting the Status Quo: The Narratives of Black Homeschoolers in Metro-Atlanta and Metro-DC." *Peabody Journal of Education* 88, no. 3 (2013): 265–83. DOI: 10.1080/0161956X.2013.79682.3.

"Fleming County Schools Homeschool Action Plan." *Fleming Country Schools*, July 17, 2018, https://www.fleming.kyschools.us/userfiles/406/my%20files/fcs homeschoolactionplanfinalboardapproved07172018.pdf?id=14722 (accessed May 19, 2020).

Gaither, Milton. *Homeschool: An American History.* New York: Palgrave Macmillan, 2008.

Gordon, Edward E., and Elaine H. Gordon. *Centuries of Tutoring: A History of Alternative Education in America and Western Europe.* Lanham, MD: University Press of America, 1990.

Granados, Alex. "Where Are North Carolina Students Going to School?" *EdNC*, July 24, 2019, https://www.ednc.org/where-are-north-carolina-students-going-to-school/ (accessed May 19, 2020).

Hertzel, June. "Literacy in the Homeschool Setting." In P. H. Dreyer (ed.), *Literacy: Building on What We Know*, pp. 60–81. Claremont, CA: Claremont Reading, 1997.

Hirsh, Aaron. "The Changing Landscape of Homeschooling in the United States." *University of Washington Center for Reinventing Public Education*, July 2019, https://www.crpe.org/sites/default/files/homeschooling_brief_final.pdf (accessed October 21, 2020).

BIBLIOGRAPHY

Homeschool Legal Defense Association. "Homeschool Laws by State." *HSLDA.org*, 2020, https://hslda.org/legal (accessed October 20, 2020).

———. "Vouchers." *NCHE.HSLDA.org*, 2020, http://nche.hslda.org/docs/nche/Issues/S/State_Vouchers.asp (accessed October 20, 2020).

Kelly, James P., and Benjamin Scafidi. "More Than Scores: An Analysis of Why and How Parents Choose Private Schools." *Friedman Foundation for Educational Choice*, November 2013, https://www.edchoice.org/wp-content/uploads/2015/07/More-Than-Scores.pdf (accessed May 19, 2020).

Kentish, Benjamin. "Labour Votes to Abolish Private Schools at Party Conference." *Independent*, September 22, 2019, https://www.independent.co.uk/news/uk/politics/labour-public-private-school-abolish-eton-vote-conference-corbyn-education-policy-a9115766.html (accessed October 21, 2020).

Kisida, Brian, Patrick Wolf, and Evan Rhinesmith. "Views from Private Schools: Attitudes about School Choice Programs in Three States." *American Enterprise Institute*, January 2015, https://www.aei.org/wp-content/uploads/2015/01/Views-from-Private-Schools-7.pdf (accessed October 21, 2020).

Levin, Yuval. *A Time to Build: From Family and Community to Congress and the Campus, How Recommitting to Our Institutions Can Revive the American Dream*. New York: Basic Books, 2020.

Liedtka, Jeanne. "Why Design Thinking Works." *Harvard Business Review*, September/October 2018, https://hbr.org/2018/09/why-design-thinking-works (accessed October 21, 2020).

Lines, Patricia M. "When Homeschoolers Go to School: A Partnership between Families and Schools." *Peabody Journal of Education* 75, no. 1–2 (2000): 159–86.

Lubienski, Christopher. "Whither the Common Good? A Critique of Homeschooling." *Peabody Journal of Education* 75, no. 1–2 (2000): 207–32.

Lyons, Linda. "Age, Religiosity, and Rural America." *Gallup*, March 11, 2003, https://news.gallup.com/poll/7960/age-religiosity-rural-america.aspx (accessed October 21, 2020).

Malkus, Nat, Cody Christensen, and Jessica Schurz. *School District Responses to the COVID-19 Pandemic: Round Six, Ending the Year of School Closures*. Washington, D.C.: American Enterprise Institute, 2020.

Malone, Clare. "Political Confession: I Think Private Schools Should Be Banned." *Fivethirtyeight*, April 29, 2019, https://fivethirtyeight.com/features/political-confessional-i-think-private-schools-should-be-banned/ (accessed October 21, 2020).

McDowell, Susan A., Annette R. Sanchez, and Susan S. Jones. "Participation and Perception: Looking at Homeschooling through a Multicultural Lens." *Peabody Journal of Education* 75, no. 1–2 (2000): 124–46. DOI: 10.1080/0161956X.2000.9681938.

McQuiggan, M., and M. Megra. "Parent and Family Involvement in Education: Results from the National Household Education Surveys Program of 2016." Washington, D.C.: U.S. Department of Education, National Center for Education

Statistics, 2017. Available at https://nces.ed.gov/pubs2017/2017102.pdf (accessed June 22, 2020).

McShane, Michael Q., and Jenn Hatfield. "Measuring Diversity in Charter School Offerings." *American Enterprise Institute*, March 1, 1988, https://www.aei.org/research-products/report/measuring-diversity-in-charter-school-offerings/ (accessed June 22, 2020).

McShane, Michael Q., Jenn Hatfield, and Elizabeth English. "The Paperwork Pile-Up: Measuring the Burden of Charter School Applications." *American Enterprise Institute*, May 19, 2015, https://www.aei.org/research-products/report/the-paperwork-pile-up-measuring-the-burden-of-charter-school-applications/?utm_source=paramount&utm_medium=email&utm_campaign=mediamcshane charterschoolapplications&utm_content=report (accessed October 20, 2020).

Michigan Office of Financial Management. "Pupil Accounting Manual 2019–20." *Michigan.gov*, 2020, https://www.michigan.gov/documents/mde/2019-20_Pupil_Accounting_Manual_672533_7.pdf (accessed October 20, 2020).

Moore, Geoffrey A. *Crossing the Chasm: Marketing and Selling Disruptive Products to Mainstream Customers*. New York: HarperBusiness, 2006.

Murphy, Joseph. *Homeschooling in America: Capturing and Assessing the Movement*. New York: Skyhorse, 2014. Originally published in 2012.

National Catholic Education Association. "Catholic School Data." *NCEA.org*, 2020, https://www.ncea.org/ncea/proclaim/catholic_school_data/catholic_school_data.aspx (accessed October 20, 2020).

National Center for Education Statistics. "Table 236.55: Total and Current Expenditures per Pupil in Public Elementary and Secondary Schools: Selected Years, 1919–20 through 2016–17." *Digest of Education Statistics*, 2019, https://nces.ed.gov/programs/digest/d19/tables/dt19_236.55.asp (accessed October 20, 2020).

———. "Table 605.10: Gross Domestic Product per Capita and Expenditures on Education Institutions per Full-Time Equivalent (FTE) Student, by Level of Education and Country: Selected Years, 2005 through 2016." *Digest of Education Statistics*, 2019, https://nces.ed.gov/programs/digest/d19/tables/dt19_605.10.asp (accessed October 20, 2020).

Nevada Homeschool Network. "Frequently Asked Questions." *Nevadahomeschoolnetwork.com*, https://nevadahomeschoolnetwork.com/faq-3/ (accessed May 19, 2020).

Papageorge, Nicholas, Seth Gershenson, and Kyung Min Kang. "Teacher Expectations Matter." *National Bureau of Education Research*, working paper 25255, November 2018, https://www.nber.org/papers/w25255.pdf (accessed October 20, 2020).

Patrick, Susan, and Chris Sturgis. "Cracking the Code: Synchronizing Policy and Practice to Support Personalized Learning." *iNACOL*, July 2011, https://files.eric.ed.gov/fulltext/ED537322.pdf (accessed October 20, 2020).

Pew Research Center. "In U.S., Decline of Christianity Continues at Rapid Pace." *Pew Research Center*, October 17, 2019, https://www.pewforum.org/2019/10/17/

in-u-s-decline-of-christianity-continues-at-rapid-pace/ (accessed October 20, 2020).

Puga, Lisa. "Homeschooling Is Our Protest: Educational Liberation for African American Homeschooling Families in Philadelphia, PA." *Peabody Journal of Education* 94, no. 3 (2019): 281–96. DOI: 10.1080/0161956X.2019.1617579.

Ray, Brian D. "A Systematic Review of the Empirical Research on Selected Aspects of Homeschooling as a School Choice." *Journal of School Choice* 11, no. 4 (2017): 604–21. DOI: 10.1080/15582159.2017.1395638.

Rogers, Everett M. *Diffusion of Innovations*. New York: Free Press, 2003.

Scruton, Roger. *How to Be a Conservative*. London: Bloomsbury, 2014.

Shanker, Albert. "National Press Club Speech: Albert Shanker, President, American Federation of Teachers Washington, D.C." *Reuther.wayne.edu*, March 31, 1988, https://reuther.wayne.edu/files/64.43.pdf (accessed October 20, 2020)

Smarick, Andy. "Can Catholic Schools Be Saved?" *National Affairs* 45 (Spring 2011). Available at https://www.nationalaffairs.com/publications/detail/can-catholic-schools-be-saved (accessed October 20, 2020).

Snyder, Thomas D. *120 Years of American Education: A Statistical Portrait*. Washington, D.C.: U.S. Department of Education, National Center for Education Statistics, 1993. Available at https://nces.ed.gov/pubs93/93442.pdf (accessed May 19, 2020).

Stern, William J. "How Dagger John Saved New York's Irish." *City Journal* (Spring 1997), https://www.city-journal.org/html/how-dagger-john-saved-new-york%E2%80%99s-irish-11934.html (accessed October 20, 2020).

Stevens, Mitchell. *Kingdom of Children: Culture and Controversy in the Homeschooling Movement*. Princeton, N.J.: Princeton University Press, 2001.

United States Supreme Court. *Pierce v. Society of Sisters* 268 U.S. 510, 1925.

U.S. Department of Education. "State Regulation of Private Schools." *Ed.gov*, 2009, https://www2.ed.gov/admins/comm/choice/regprivschl/regprivschl.pdf (accessed October 20, 2020).

Vermont Agency of Education. "Home Study Frequently Asked Questions: Public School." *Education.vermont.gov*, February 18, 2020, https://education.vermont.gov/documents/home-study-faq-public-school (accessed May 19, 2020).

Wang, K., A. Rathbun, and L. Musu. *School Choice in the United States: 2019*. Washington, D.C.: U.S. Department of Education, National Center for Education Statistics, 2019. Available at https://nces.ed.gov/pubs2019/2019106.pdf (accessed May 19, 2020).Wearne, Eric. "A Survey of Families in a Charter Hybrid Homeschool." *Peabody Journal of Education* 94, no. 3 (2019): 297–311.

West, Robin L. "The Harms of Homeschooling." *Philosophy and Public Policy Quarterly* 29, no. 3–4 (2009): 7–12.

Wixom, Micah Ann. "State Homeschool Policies: A Patchwork of Provisions." *Education Commission of the States*, July 2015, https://www.ecs.org/clearinghouse/01/20/42/12042.pdf (accessed May 19, 2020).

INDEX

AB 1505, 81
AB 1507, 81
Alliance Christian Academy, 61, 72
Ambleside Method, 30, 100, 109
APEX Homeschool Program, 40
Augustine Academy, 29–30, 32, 96, 100, 109

Bartholet, Elizabeth, 23–24
Berrien Springs, 36, 71

Calvert Homeschool, 33
Capitol Hill Learning Group, 60, 61, 95, 98
Carnegie Unit, 54, 77
Carney, Tim, 111
Catholic schools, 6, 17, 37, 57–59
charter schools, 4–6, 36–37, 44, 46, 49, 102, 110; authorizing of, 79–82; design thinking in, 90–91; part-time enrollment in, 78–79
Christian Liberty Academic School System (CLASS), 33
Christ Preparatory Academy, 2, 65, 83

Choices Charter School, 91
Classical Christian Conservatory of Alexandria, 43, 62, 95, 109
classical-model education, 15, 37, 43, 57, 59, 65, 76, 99, 109, 120, 121
Clonlara School, 34
competency-based frameworks, 72, 76–78
cottage schools, 33, 38
COVID-19, 2, 3, 108, 109, 121

Dame school, 33
Da Vinci Connect, 37, 102, 105–106, 109
design thinking, 90–93
Dwyer, James G., and Peters, Shawn F., 16–17, 24

EdChoice, 14, 49
Educational Response Longitudinal Survey, 3
education savings account, 82–83, 84–86
Epic Charter schools, 47

Fleming County Schools, 35, 76–78, 112
Freeman, Barbara, 38–40, 76

Gaither, Milton, 15–17, 34–35
Gordon, Edward E., and Elaine H., 14
Grace Prep, 38–40, 76
Gull Lake Community Schools and Virtual Partnership, 12

Hallmark Charter School, 36–37, 90–91
Hertzel, June, 22
Holt, John, 18, 34
homeschooling co-ops, 4, 32, 34–35, 39, 74, 76
Home School Legal Defense Association (HSLDA), 18–19, 73–74, 83, 121
Hughes, "Dagger John", 6

Julian Charter Schools, 60, 81

Legacy Classical Christian Academy, 63, 64, 109
Levin, Yuval, 51, 111
Liedtka, Jeanne, 91–92
Lighthouse Christian, 2
Lubienski, Christopher, 23–24

Mann, Horace, 63
Mason, Charlotte, 30, 100
Moore, Geoffrey, 98–99
Moore, Raymond and Dorothy, 18
Mountain Phoenix Community School, 65, 102, 109
Murphy, Joseph, 13, 20, 31

National Center for Education Statistics (NCES), 19, 21
National Homeschool Football Association, 2
NAUMS, 39–40

part-time public school enrollment, 8, 35, 36, 71–72, 78–79
private school, 4–6, 17, 36–38, 44–45, 84–85, 99, 102, 107, 120; choice programs and, 82–83; regulation and, 71–72, 74–76; special education and, 53; teaching in, 60–62, 65–67; tuition and, 48–49, 84

Ray, Brian, 24–25
Rogers, Everett, 93–96, 98

school spending, 5
Scruton, Sir Roger, 52
Stevens, Mitchell, 17–18, 34, 90
St. John Paul II Preparatory School, 57–58, 63
Summit Academy, 64

tax credit scholarships, 82, 83, 85
Tebow, Tim, 35

UMSI, 39–40, 76, 122

Vision Charter School, 59
vouchers, 82–83, 85

Waldorf-model education, 66, 76, 99, 100, 102, 108, 109
Wearne, Eric, 44–45
West, Robin, 23

ABOUT THE AUTHOR

Michael Q. McShane is director of national research at EdChoice. He is editor of *New and Better Schools* (Rowman & Littlefield, 2015); author of *Education and Opportunity* (2014); and coeditor of *Bush–Obama School Reform: Lessons Learned* (2018), *No Longer Forgotten: The Triumphs and Struggles of Rural Education in America* (Rowman & Littlefield, 2018), *Failure Up Close: What Happens, Why It Happens, and What We Can Learn from It* (Rowman & Littlefield, 2018), *Educational Entrepreneurship Today* (2016), *Teacher Quality 2.0* (2014), and *Common Core Meets Education Reform* (2013). McShane is an opinion contributor to *Forbes*, and his analyses and commentary have been published widely in the media, including in *USA Today*, the *Washington Post*, and the *Wall Street Journal*. He has also been featured in such education-specific outlets as *Teachers College Record*, *Education Week*, *Phi Delta Kappan*, and *Education Next*. In addition to authoring numerous white papers, McShane has had academic work published in *Education Finance and Policy*, *The Handbook of Education Politics and Policy*, and the *Journal of School Choice*. A former high school teacher, he earned a Ph.D. in education policy from the University of Arkansas, a M.Ed. from the University of Notre Dame, and a B.A. in English from St. Louis University. He is also an adjunct fellow in education policy studies at the American Enterprise Institute and a senior fellow at the Show-Me Institute.

www.ingramcontent.com/pod-product-compliance
Lightning Source LLC
Chambersburg PA
CBHW020749230426
43665CB00009B/541